With love and gratitude to my beloved wife Nancy
and our children
Jonathon, Bridget, Timothy, Hillary, Maximilian, Madeline,
Judith, Augustine, Theodore, Rebecca and Stephen.

Other Books by Patrick Madrid

Answer Me This!

Any Friend of God's Is a Friend of Mine

More Catholic Than the Pope

A Pocket Guide to Catholic Apologetics

Pope Fiction

Search and Rescue

Surprised by Truth

Surprised by Truth 2

Surprised by Truth 3

Where Is That in the Bible?

Why Is That in Tradition?

Does the Bible Really Say That?

Discovering Catholic Teaching in Scripture

Patrick Madrid

SERVANT
BOOKS

PUBLISHED BY ST. ANTHONY MESSENGER PRESS
CINCINNATI, OHIO

English translation of the *Catechism of the Catholic Church* for the United States of America Copyright © 1994, United States Catholic Conference, Inc.—Libreria Editrice Vaticana. English translation of the: *Catechism of the Catholic Church Modifications from the Editio Typica* Copyright © 1997, United States Catholic Conference, Inc.—Libreria Editrice Vaticana. Used with permission.

Unless otherwise noted, Scripture passages have been taken from the *Revised Standard Version*, Catholic edition. Copyright 1946, 1952, 1971 by the Division of Christian Education of the National Council of the Churches of Christ in the USA. Used by permission. All rights reserved.

Cover design by Candle Light Studios
Cover photography: Photodisc/B. Meredith
Book design by Phillips Robinette, O.F.M.

LIBRARY OF CONGRESS CATALOGING-IN-PUBLICATION DATA

Madrid, Patrick, 1960-
  Does the Bible really say that? : discovering Catholic teaching in Scripture / Patrick Madrid.
     p. cm.
  Includes bibliographical references and index.
   ISBN 0-86716-774-2 (pbk. : alk. paper) 1. Catholic Church—Apologetic works. 2. Bible—Criticism, interpretation, etc. I. Title.

BX1752.M237 2006
230'.2—dc22

                        2006009392

ISBN-13: 978-0-86716-774-0
ISBN-10: 0-86716-774-2

Published by Servant Books, an imprint of
St. Anthony Messenger Press
28 W. Liberty St.
Cincinnati, OH 45202
www.ServantBooks.org

Printed in the United States of America.
Printed on acid-free paper.

08 09 10 5 4 3

Contents

Introduction

Saint Jerome, one of the Catholic Church's greatest Scripture scholars, once remarked that "Ignorance of the Scriptures is ignorance of Christ [St. Jerome, *Commentariorum in Isaiam libri xviii* prol.: PL 24, 17b]" (*Catechism of the Catholic Church* [*CCC*], 133).[1] That is bad enough. But to be ignorant of one's ignorance is even worse.

And yet many Catholics do neglect to read and study the Bible. Too often Sacred Scripture can be reduced to a mere prop, a religious symbol of God's authority that has little to do with one's daily life. True, most Catholic households have at least one Bible on hand; but it's also true that, generally speaking, it goes unread.

This is what Saint Jerome meant when he warned about the danger of being ignorant of Scripture. When through laziness or some other excuse we ignore or neglect to study and ponder God's written Word, we find ourselves cut off from a major source of information about Jesus Christ—who he is, what he did for us and why we should have faith in him, love him and obey his teachings (Luke 6:46). Sacred Scripture reveals all these things for us.

Each Sunday, in Catholic parishes everywhere, an interesting ritual plays out at Mass. At the proclamation of the Gospel, the priest or deacon processes to the pulpit with great solemnity and drama, holding the lectionary aloft. Often, incense is used to show forth the sacred importance of the Gospel reading. The congregation then stands when the Gospel is proclaimed. And this is all as it should be. The holding aloft of the lectionary, the incense, the standing to show reverence—these are all outward signs of an inward reality: namely, that what is contained in Scripture is extremely sacred and important and should be given the utmost attention.

But here is the great irony. Is it not true that, apart from that ceremonial moment at Mass when all the outward signs betoken Scripture's importance, many, if not most, lay Catholics pay very little attention to the Bible outside of Mass?

The good news is that this sad and needless ignorance of Scripture among lay Catholics can be overcome, for the most part swiftly and effortlessly, simply by reading the Bible every day, even for just a few minutes.

Not only will reading Scripture daily enrich and nourish your soul, but it will provide you with solid answers to many of life's most urgent questions. Reading Scripture will deepen your prayer life and strengthen the effects of the sacraments in your soul; it will help you understand and get along better with others; it will encourage and assist you in curbing your appetites and controlling your emotions. When questions and challenges come your way, as they inevitably will, Scripture will prepare and equip you to speak about your beliefs as a Christian more clearly and confidently, without agitation. Best of all, reading the Bible regularly will dramatically deepen your love for and knowledge of Jesus Christ.

And so, with these marvelous goals in mind, I present for you here a series of biblical discussions on a variety of issues that Catholics everywhere face. My hope is that this book will help you jump-start the process of becoming familiar (or simply more familiar) with the truth of Christ as it is unfolded for us so beautifully in the pages of Scripture.

My only advice is this: Never forget that reading this book *about* the Bible should never replace reading the Bible itself.

1

Buddy, Can You Spare a Dime?

Bob Hope used to say, "If you don't have charity in your heart, you have the worst kind of heart trouble." With that astute observation in mind, let's consider Scripture's teachings on charity toward our neighbor in the form of giving.

All too easily, a kind of creeping selfishness can invade our hectic lives without our even knowing it, crowded as our days are with a multitude of "me-oriented" busyness. How often do we go out of our way to help others? True, most of us donate here and there to "worthy causes," but don't we usually give to organizations that send us a "love gift" in return or, at the very least, provide us with the ever-popular tax deduction? Few of us give alms to people who can do nothing for us in return.

Christ's exhortation to "do good" to our neighbor is *person-specific*. Yes, we should contribute to worthy charitable organizations, and of course we must do what we can to assist the local Church financially (parish and diocese), but we're primarily called to help *people*—the poor and disadvantaged, the homeless and friendless, strangers, unwed mothers—indeed, anyone who lacks the physical necessities of life. In Matthew 25:31–46, Christ says he will return as Judge to reward the "sheep" and condemn the "goats" based on how they (meaning you and I) assisted or failed to assist the "least" of their brothers and sisters with food, shelter, clothing, water and other basic needs. Ask yourself: On that day, will you be one of the sheep or one of the goats?

Let these Bible passages animate your zeal for helping others, especially through almsgiving—giving money to those who legitimately need it more than you do:

Tobit 4:7–11 "Give alms from your possessions to all who live uprightly, and do not let your eye begrudge the gift when you make it. Do not turn your face away from any poor man, and the face of God will not be turned away from you. If you have many possessions, make your gift from them in proportion; if few, do not be afraid to give according to the little you have. So you will be laying up a good treasure for yourself against the day of necessity. For charity delivers from death and keeps you from entering the darkness; and for all who practice it charity is an excellent offering in the presence of the Most High."

Luke 12:33 "Sell your possessions, and give alms; provide yourselves with purses that do not grow old, with a treasure in the heavens that does not fail, where no thief approaches and no moth destroys. For where your treasure is, there will your heart be also."

2 Corinthians 9:10–12 "He who supplies seed to the sower and bread for food will supply and multiply your resources and increase the harvest of your righteousness. You will be enriched in every way for great generosity, which through us will produce thanksgiving to God; for the rendering of this service not only supplies the wants of the saints but also overflows in many thanksgivings to God."

Hebrews 13:16 "[D]o not neglect to do good and to share what you have, for such sacrifices are pleasing to God."

Being generous is the first part of true charity that pleases God. The second part is just as important: to not be showy or self-serving in your giving. Christ said, "Beware of practicing your piety before men in order to be seen by them; for then you will have no reward from your Father who is in heaven. Thus, when you give alms, sound no trumpet before you, as the hypocrites do in the synagogues and in the streets, that they may be praised by men. Truly, I say to you, they have their reward. But when you give alms, do not let your left hand know what your right hand is doing, so that your alms may be in secret; and your Father who sees in secret will reward you" (Matthew 6:1–4).

Saint James said, "What does it profit, my brethren, if a man says he has faith but has not works? Can his faith save him? If a brother or sister is ill-clad and in lack of daily food, and one of you says to them, 'Go in peace, be warmed and filled,' without giving them the things needed for the body, what does it profit? So faith by itself, if it has no works, is dead" (James 2:14–17).

And in Acts 20:35: "In all things I have shown you that by so toiling one must help the weak, remembering the words of the Lord Jesus, how he said, 'It is more blessed to give than to receive.'"

In Luke 10:29–37 we find the parable of the Good Samaritan, who gave aid and comfort and alms to a total stranger. It's a story you surely know by heart, but has its meaning sunk *into* your heart? Read that passage prayerfully, and remember Christ's command to "Go and do likewise."

Further Reading: Sirach 3:30–31; 17:20–23; 40:14;
Tobit 12:8–10; Psalm 37:21; Matthew 5:38–42; Mark 12:38–44;
Acts 10:1–2; 1 Timothy 6:17–19; James 1:27

2

Temptations

The famous wit Samuel Johnson once wrote, "If you are idle, be not solitary; if you are solitary be not idle."[1] He knew, as we all do from bitter experience, that temptations to sin are most formidable when we're alone and think no one will see. But of course, *God* sees, though we try to ignore that reality.

King David reflected on this fact: "O LORD, thou hast searched me and known me! / Thou knowest when I sit down and when I rise up; / thou discernest my thoughts from afar. / Thou searchest out my path and my lying down, / and art acquainted with all my ways. / Even before a word is on my tongue, / lo, O LORD, thou knowest it altogether" (Psalm 139:1–4).

So, since we know we gain nothing from rebelling against God through sin, and since no sin, however clandestine, is hidden from God, why does he allow us to be tempted in the first place?

The *Catechism of the Catholic Church* explains that this is part of our progress toward spiritual maturity enabling us to "*discern* between trials, which are necessary for the growth of the inner man, [cf. *Lk.* 8:13-15; *Acts* 14:22; *Rom* 5:3-5; *2 Tim* 3:12] and temptation, which leads to sin and death [cf. *Jas* 1:14-15]." The Holy Spirit also gives us the grace necessary to distinguish between "*being* tempted and *consenting* to temptation" (CCC, 2847).

As Scripture warns, temptations are "a delight to the eyes"

(Genesis 3:6). And though they are highly attractive, at least at first, in reality they are a downward-sloping path to eternal destruction. "There is a way which seems right to a man, but its end is the way to death" (Proverbs 14:12).

We must guard against temptation, first, so we won't commit sin and, second, so we won't become a source of temptation to others, causing them to sin because of us. Christ warned, "Woe to the world for temptations to sin! For it is necessary that temptations come, but woe to the man by whom the temptation comes!" (Matthew 18:7).

When Christ taught us the "Our Father," he included the petition "lead us not into temptation" (Matthew 6:13). The *Catechism* explains what this means:

> [O]ur sins result from our consenting to temptation; we therefore ask our Father not to "lead" us into temptation. It is difficult to translate the Greek verb used by a single English word: the Greek means both "do not allow us to enter into temptation" and "do not let us yield to temptation" [cf. *Mt*. 26:41]. "God cannot be tempted by evil and he himself tempts no one"; [*Jas* 1:3] on the contrary, he wants to set us free from evil. We ask him not to allow us to take the way that leads to sin. (*CCC*, 2846; see also 2863, emphasis added)

James 1:12–15 says: "Blessed is the man who endures trial, for when he has stood the test he will receive the crown of life which God has promised to those who love him. Let no one say when he is tempted, 'I am tempted by God'; for God cannot be tempted with evil and he himself tempts no one; but each person is tempted when he is lured and enticed by his own desire. Then desire when it has conceived gives birth to sin; and sin when it is full-grown brings forth death" (see Romans 6:23).

And Saint Paul wrote about his bafflement at his own struggles with temptation and sin:

> I do not understand my own actions. For I do not do what I want, but I do the very thing I hate.... I can will what is right, but I cannot do it. For I do not do the good I want, but the evil I do not want is what I do.... I find it to be a law that when I want to do right, evil lies close at hand. For I delight in the law of God, in my inmost self, but I see in my members another law at war with the law of my mind and making me captive to the law of sin which dwells in my members (Romans 7:15, 18–19, 21–24; see 7:13–14).

If even Saint Paul had to contend with unruly passions and temptations, we are in excellent company as we struggle against the temptations that nip and peck at us.

We must avoid the near occasions of sin that give rise to temptations (Matthew 18:8–9) and proactively seek to conquer temptations through prayer and by cultivating virtue. "Why do you sleep?" Christ admonishes us. "Rise and pray that you may not enter into temptation" (Luke 22:46; see 22:39–45).

Satan tempted Christ himself during his forty-day fast in the desert (Luke 4:1–13). Christ is the perfect model of how we should react when the devil dangles a sinful enticement before us. We must rely on God's grace for strength to conquer it (2 Corinthians 12:7–9), for his grace is stronger than any temptation, however formidable.

Remember what Saint Paul said in 1 Corinthians 10:13: "No temptation has overtaken you that is not common to man. God is faithful, and he will not let you be tempted beyond your strength, but with the temptation will also provide the way of escape, that you may be able to endure it." When temptations come your way, pray for strength and remember these encouraging words: "I can do all things in him who strengthens me" (Philippians 4:13).

Further Reading: Genesis 3:1–24; Psalm 121; Matthew 4:1–17; Luke 8:4–15; 1 Corinthians 7:1–7; 10:13; Hebrews 2:18
CCC, 538–556, 1262, 1520, 2340, 2848

3

Do Catholics Worship Statues?

When I arrived one evening at a suburban Chicago parish to conduct an apologetics seminar, I noticed a life-sized statue of Our Lady of Fatima on the rectory lawn. Three smaller statues of Lucia, Francisco and Jacinta, the children to whom Our Lady appeared, knelt in prayer, heads bowed, before the larger statue.

Turning to my colleague in the car, I joked, "What a great religion Catholicism is! Not only can we worship statues, but our *statues* can worship statues." We chuckled at the absurdity of the thought.

When I mentioned this incident during the seminar, the Catholics in the audience laughed at the notion of statues worshiping statues as much as at the nonsense of humans worshiping statues—but some of the Protestants in attendance weren't laughing. They looked puzzled. The reason, as I discovered during the question and answer session, was that some of them actually believed that Catholics *do* worship statues.

The suspicion that Catholics engage in idolatry fuels this Protestant disapproval of Catholic statues and images. And the concern is far more widespread than you might think. Their scriptural objection to religious statues is primarily based on two passages: In Exodus 20:3–5, God warns Moses, "You shall have no other gods before me. You shall not make for yourself a graven image, or any likeness of anything that is in heaven above, or that is in the earth beneath, or that is in the water under the earth; you shall not bow down to them or serve them" (see Deuteronomy 5:6–9). And Deuteronomy 27:15 says, "Cursed be the man who makes a graven or molten image, an abomination to the LORD, a thing made by the hands of a craftsman, and sets it up in secret."

Indeed, admonitions against idolatry appear throughout Scripture (Numbers 33:52; Deuteronomy 7:5, 25; 9:12; 12:3; 2 Kings 17:9–18; 23:24; 2 Chronicles 23:17; 28:1–3; 33:18–25; 34:1–7). In 1 Corinthians 10:14 Saint Paul clearly admonishes, "[B]eloved, shun the worship of idols" (see Romans 1:18–23).

Keep in mind that God condemns worshiping any *thing* as an idol, whether it be a statue, or stock options, or sex, or power or a new car. But he does not prohibit religious images, provided they are used properly. For example, in Exodus 25, God commands Moses to carve religious statues:

> The LORD said to Moses…"[Y]ou shall make two cherubim of gold; of hammered work shall you make them, on the two ends of the mercy seat. Make one cherub on the one end, and one cherub on the other end; of one piece with the mercy seat shall you make the cherubim on its two ends. The cherubim shall spread out their wings above, overshadowing the mercy seat with their wings, their faces one to another; toward the mercy seat shall the faces of the cherubim be." (Exodus 25:1, 18–20; see 26:1)

It is evident from this passage and others that there are circumstances in which religious images are not merely permissible, but are actually *pleasing* to God.

In Exodus 28:33–34 the Lord commands that Aaron's priestly vestments be adorned with images of pomegranates. In Numbers 21:8–9 he commands Moses to fashion a graven image of a snake that would miraculously cure poisonous snakebites (a mysterious foreshadowing of the cross of Christ [John 3:14; 8:28]). Yet in 2 Kings 18:4, when the people begin *worshiping* the bronze serpent, the king immediately destroys it. What once was a legitimate sacred image had become an object of idolatry—a cautionary tale for anyone tempted toward that sin. There is also an oddly humorous incident involving images described in 1 Samuel 6:1–18.

And notice what God told Solomon as he constructed the temple: "'Concerning this house which you are building, *if you will walk in my statutes and obey my ordinances and keep all my commandments and walk in them*, then I will establish my word with you, which I spoke to David your father. And I will dwell among the children of Israel, and will not forsake my people Israel.' So Solomon built the house, and finished it" (1 Kings 6:12–14, emphasis added).

This passage contains crucial insight into the use of religious images, for Solomon's temple contained many statues and graven images, including angels, trees, flowers, oxen and lions (1 Kings 6:23–35; 7:25, 36). Solomon's decision to include these religious images came from the gift of wisdom with which God had blessed him (1 Kings 3:1–28). Far from being displeased, God said to Solomon: "I have heard your prayer and your supplication, which you have made before me; I have consecrated this house, which you have built, and put my name there for ever; my eyes and my heart will be there for all time" (1 Kings 9:3).

Obviously, God would not have blessed Solomon and "consecrated" his temple filled with statues and images if he did not approve of them—further evidence that images can be good when used to order our minds toward heavenly realities.

In the New Testament, Christ is called "the image of the

invisible God" (Colossians 1:15). The Greek word here for "image" is *eikon*, from which we derive the word "icon."

Just as we keep pictures of our family and friends to remind us of them, we also keep religious statues and images in our homes and churches to remind us of Christ, Our Lady and the saints.

Further Reading: John 14:9; Colossians 1:15; Hebrews 1:3; 1 John 1:1–3
CCC, 1159–1161, 2112–2114, 2129–2141

4

Calling Priests "Father"

The Catholic custom of addressing priests as "father" dates back to the early years of Christianity. The writings of the early Church Fathers brim with examples of priests, bishops and popes being referred to as "father." In fact, the term "pope" derives from the Latin *papa*, an affectionate form of address given to many bishops in the early Church, although now, in the Western Church, it refers specifically to the Bishop of Rome.

The Bible, however, seems to contradict this ancient Catholic practice, and many Bible-believing non-Catholics consider calling priests "father" to be a direct violation of Christ's instruction in Matthew 23:9: "[C]all no man your father on earth, for you have one Father, who is in heaven." At first glance, those sixteen words seem to cinch the case against this longstanding Catholic custom. But let's look deeper and see if that's really the case.

The truth is that Christ did not *literally* mean call no one "teacher," "father" or "master." If he had, we would expect to see the Apostles follow this literal interpretation throughout the New Testament, but in fact we see exactly the opposite: the New Testament writers frequently called men "father," as well as "teacher" and "master" (Acts 5:34; Colossians 4:1; 2 Timothy 1:11). This indicates their understanding that Christ's words in this case were not to be taken literally.

Rather, it seems that Christ was warning us not to look to any human authority as our teacher, father or master in the same way that we would look to God to fulfill those roles in our lives. The Lord's admonition was prompted here by his disgust with the Pharisees and scribes, who had wrongfully arrogated to themselves some things reserved to God alone (Matthew 15:1–9; Mark 7:6–13). For more on this problem, see chapter five.

Catholics are not violating Christ's instructions by calling priests "father." The first clue is that Christ, who is God himself, is utterly incapable by his divine nature of contradicting or somehow being at odds with the two other Persons of the Blessed Trinity, the Father and the Holy Spirit. "God is not a God of confusion but of peace" (1 Corinthians 14:33). Therefore, when we encounter episodes in Scripture where the Holy Spirit inspires people to use the word "father" as a form of address, we can safely conclude that Christ's words in Matthew 23 cannot have meant literally "do not call priests 'father'."

For example, in Acts 7:2 Saint Stephen addresses the Jewish elders as "[b]rethren and fathers." Stephen was "full of the Holy Spirit" when he uttered these words to *the very same men* Christ rebuked in Matthew 23 (Acts 7:55; see 6:8). Throughout his soliloquy, Stephen repeatedly referred to various men in the Old Testament as "fathers."

Ask yourself: If Christ had meant "call no man 'father'" literally, then how could the Holy Spirit have inspired Stephen to address his audience as "fathers," as well as inspire Saint Luke to record this speech so favorably in the book of Acts? Clearly, he would not have if, in fact, Christ had meant his comments in Matthew 23 literally.

Saint John repeatedly addresses men as "fathers" in 1 John (2:13–14). Saint Paul also addresses the Jewish leaders of his day as "fathers" in Acts 22:1. He uses the title "father" when writing about Abraham in passages such as Romans 4:17–18. And in 1 Thessalonians 2:11 he describes his ministry among the Christians in Thessalonica as "a father with his children."

And then there's Saint Paul's statement in 1 Corinthians 4:14–16: "I do not write this to make you ashamed, but to admonish you as my beloved children. For though you have countless guides in Christ, you do not have many fathers. *For I became your father in Christ Jesus through the gospel.* I urge you, then, be imitators of me" (emphasis added).

Again we see in these Scriptures that calling priests "father" is not contrary to Christ's teaching. After all, Saint Paul urges us to imitate him in doing so. Here we also see why this venerable Christian practice came into being in the first place: Priests are indeed our spiritual fathers. Priests "give birth" to us spiritually through the waters of baptism (John 3:3–5; Titus 3:5), they nourish us with the Body and Blood of Christ in the Holy Eucharist (1 Corinthians 11:23–32) and they care for us and bind our spiritual wounds through the healing sacraments of baptism, confession and the anointing of the sick (John 20:20–23; 2 Corinthians 5:18–19; James 5:13–16). Priests shepherd their flocks with all the fatherly love and concern that any good human father has for his own family. It makes perfect biblical sense to call priests "father."

Finally, notice that many who quote Matthew 23:9 against Catholics often overlook verses 8 and 10: "But you are not to be called rabbi, for you have one teacher, and you are all brethren.... Neither be called masters, for you have one master, the Christ." You see, if Catholics are violating Christ's command in verse 9, then any Protestant minister who uses the title "doctor" (*doctor* is a Latin word for "teacher") is just as guilty. Dr. Jerry Falwell, Dr. Billy Graham, and Dr. D. James Kennedy are prominent examples of such ministers. Similarly, any Christian with a master's degree is in trouble!

5

Sacred Tradition

Tradition is a "red flag" word for many non-Catholics. They see in Christ's condemnation of the "tradition of men" (Mark 7:1–13; Matthew 15:1–9) a wholesale condemnation of *all* tradition. But this is a misunderstanding of what he meant when he spoke about traditions of men which "ma[k]e void the word of God."

The Pharisees concocted certain "traditions" to avoid following God's laws. The best example is the one Christ condemned in Matthew 15, the so-called "Korban rule." Under this scheme, Jews could "donate" all their money to the temple treasury as a pious act of almsgiving. This would afford them the excuse of being "unable" to help should their poor or infirm parents approach them in need of assistance (although they actually had full access to their funds).

To callously ignore your parents' needs would violate God's command to "honor your father and mother" (Exodus 20:12). So, under the Korban rule, someone who had technically donated all of his money to God would have a "legitimate" excuse not to give money to his parents. The chicanery of this "tradition of men" is obvious, as is the reason why Christ would condemn that tradition as corrupt and contrary to God's justice.

But not all tradition is bad.

The fact is, the canon of the New Testament is part of God's revelation to the Church. But that revelation didn't come to the

Church in the pages of Scripture, the written Word of God. Rather, God gradually revealed this all-important information to the Church through a different means, completely outside of Scripture. After all, there is no "inspired table of contents" in the Bible telling us which books belong in it.

This revelation was preserved and faithfully taught by the Catholic Church, transmitted in its integrity from one generation to the next. That's why we Catholics have the same twenty-seven books in our New Testaments—from Matthew to Revelation— that Protestants, Mormons and Jehovah's Witnesses have in theirs. They have these books in their Bibles because, like it or not, whether they are aware of it or not (and very few of them are aware of it), it was the Catholic Church that received from God the revelation that these books are inspired (see 2 Timothy 3:16), and over the next few centuries the Church fixed the exact canon of these books.

"How can you Catholics believe in purgatory or the Immaculate Conception?" they ask with a roll of their eyes. "Those teachings are nowhere taught in the Bible. Worse yet, they're traditions of men (see Matthew 15:1–9; Mark 7:1–13; Colossians 2:8; Ephesians 4:14), unbiblical teachings that go against what God says in the Bible." This attitude is common among Protestants, and you're likely to run into it, so it's important that you know what to say about Tradition—what it is, what it isn't, what it does and why we need it.

For many Protestants, "Tradition" connotes the worst sort of man-made traditions, the kind Christ warned against in Mark 7:1–13 and Matthew 15:1–9. They see Catholic traditions, such as the Real Presence, infant baptism and purgatory, as prime examples of man-made doctrines that conflict with Scripture. Based on the Reformation principle of *sola scriptura*, they argue that Catholics have *added* things to Scripture, something they consider to be a major no-no.

Many would say that Catholic traditions are bad not simply because they are "added" to the Bible but, worse yet, because they feel they are in direct conflict with it.

It's important, therefore, to understand what Catholic Tradition is and what it is not, so we can see that not all tradition conflicts with Scripture. In fact, when one correctly understands Tradition, it not only ceases to be a stumbling block but can even become a stepping-stone to the Catholic Church. Many converts to Catholicism have told me this was their experience once they encountered a Catholic who was willing and able to explain authentic Tradition using Scripture.

Let's return again to Saint Paul, who gives us a theological mini-treatise on the nature and purpose of Tradition, right in the pages of Scripture: "Now I would remind you, brethren, in what terms I preached to you the gospel, which you received, in which you stand, by which you are saved, if you hold it fast—unless you believed in vain. For I delivered to you as of first importance what I also received, that Christ died for our sins in accordance with the scriptures" (1 Corinthians 15:1–3).

Notice the words Saint Paul chose:

✢ there is a body of teaching that "you received" (Greek: *parelabete*);

✢ he "preached" this teaching (Greek: *euangelion*);

✢ we are to "hold it fast," meaning that we are not permitted to neglect or dispense with this oral teaching (see also 2 Thessalonians 2:15);

✢ he "received" this oral teaching first and then "delivered" (Greek: *paredoka*) this teaching orally to his readers (which

is the precise meaning of Tradition: receiving it and handing it on);

✢ this orally transmitted teaching is "in accordance with" and
compliments the teaching of Scripture, just as it is a sure
interpretation of what it reflects in Scripture (i.e., the inextri-
cable link between Scripture and Tradition).

Here Saint Paul, one of the Church's first bishops and doctors,
functions in his capacity as a member of the *magisterium*, or "teaching office," of the Church: to explain the meaning of Scripture and
faithfully deliver the message to the faithful (Matthew 28:19–20).

1 Corinthians 15 provides us with an excellent biblical back-
drop for understanding how it is that Sacred Tradition works in
the Church—alongside, and never in competition with, Sacred
Scripture.

Further Reading: Luke 1:1–4; 1 Corinthians 11:2;
2 Thessalonians 2:15
CCC, 75–100

6

Divorce and Remarriage

Divorce and remarriage is a widespread problem these days. Many Christians know the pain of divorce, and some have remarried. Not surprisingly, many of them wonder about the spiritual ramifications of their situation.

Divorced Christians who have never attempted remarriage or who have received from the Church what is known as an "annulment" are not the focus here. Rather, it's Christians who divorce and remarry without going through the annulment process who should heed the danger of their spiritual situation.

The Catholic Church's teaching on divorce and remarriage is anchored squarely on Christ's teaching: "Every one who divorces his wife and marries another commits adultery, and he who marries a woman divorced from her husband commits adultery" (Luke 16:18). And again:

> It was also said, "Whoever divorces his wife, let him give her a certificate of divorce." But I say to you that every one who divorces his wife, except on the ground of unchastity, makes her an adulteress; and whoever marries a divorced woman commits adultery. (Matthew 5:31–32)

The *Catechism* says:

> *Divorce* is a grave offense against the natural law. It claims to break the contract, to which the spouses freely consented, to live with each other till death. Divorce does injury to the covenant of salvation, of which sacramental marriage is the sign. Contracting a new union, even if it is recognized by civil law, adds to the gravity of the rupture: the remarried spouse is then in a situation of public and permanent adultery....
>
> Divorce is immoral also because it introduces disorder into the family and into society. This disorder brings grave harm to the deserted spouse, to children traumatized by the separation of their parents and often torn between them, and because of its contagious effect which makes it truly a plague on society.
>
> It can happen that one of the spouses is the innocent victim of a divorce decreed by civil law; this spouse therefore has not contravened the moral law. There is a considerable difference between a spouse who has sincerely tried to be faithful to the sacrament of marriage and is unjustly abandoned, and one who through his own grave fault destroys a canonically valid marriage [cf. FC 84]. (CCC, 2384–2386)

This is why God said, "I hate divorce.... So take heed to yourselves and do not be faithless" (Malachi 2:16).

When the rich young man asked Christ what he must do to go to heaven, he responded, "If you would enter life, keep the commandments." Among those he listed was "You shall not commit adultery" (Matthew 19:16–19).

And in Matthew 19:3–10, when the Pharisees tested Christ by asking, "Is it lawful to divorce one's wife for any cause?" Christ answered:

Have you not read that he who made them from the beginning made them male and female, and said,"For this reason a man shall leave his father and mother and be joined to his wife, and the two shall become one"? So they are no longer two but one. What therefore God has joined together, let no man put asunder. They said to him,"Why then did Moses command one to give a certificate of divorce, and to put her away?" He said to them, "For your hardness of heart Moses allowed you to divorce your wives, but from the beginning it was not so. And I say to you: whoever divorces his wife, except for unchastity, and marries another, commits adultery."

Some argue that the phrase "except for unchastity" constitutes an "exception clause" that allows for divorce and remarriage in cases where one or both spouses commits adultery. But this is a misreading of the text. The Greek word here for unchastity, *porneia*, refers to sexual unlawfulness in which two "spouses" are not validly married (John 4:17–18), though they live as if they were. In such cases, to separate and then marry someone else would not constitute adultery, since the two parties were not really married in God's eyes (i.e. sacramentally) in the first place.

A valid marriage, however, cannot be dissolved. As Christ said, "They are no longer two but one. What therefore God has joined together, let no man put asunder."

Saint Paul added, "[A] married woman is bound by law to her husband as long as he lives; but if her husband dies she is discharged from the law concerning the husband. Accordingly, she will be called an adulteress if she lives with another man while her husband is alive. But if her husband dies she is free from that law, and if she marries another man she is not an adulteress" (Romans 7:2–3).

Anyone who imagines that divorce and remarriage is not serious in God's eyes should ponder this warning: "Do you not know that the unrighteous will not inherit the kingdom of God? Do not be deceived; neither the immoral, nor idolaters, nor adulterers, nor homosexuals, nor thieves, nor the greedy, nor drunkards, nor revilers, nor robbers will inherit the kingdom of God" (1 Corinthians 6:9–10).

That passage might trouble someone who is divorced and remarried but never went through the annulment process, receiving from the Church a declaration of nullity (i.e., "an annulment"). If so, he or she *should* feel troubled. His conscience is warning that something is spiritually very wrong.

If you are in this situation, contact a priest for sacramental confession and get advice on how to correct things—before it's too late.

Further Reading: Exodus 20:14; Leviticus 20:10; Deuteronomy 5:18; Proverbs 6:32; Malachi 3:5; Matthew 5:27–28; Mark 10:11–12; 17–19; Luke 18:19–20; Romans 2:22; 13:8–10; 1 Corinthians 7:10–11; Hebrews 13:4 CCC, 1629–1651, 2384–2386

7

Gossip, Slander and Judging People's Hearts

Mark Twain once wrote, "It takes your enemy and your friend, working together, to hurt you: the one to slander you, and the other to get the news to you."[1] How right he was.

There are few things in life more painful than being the target of mean-spirited comments. Most of us know from experience how devastating the weapon of an unbridled tongue can be. Whether one is on the giving end or the receiving end, we know how deeply gossip, slander and detraction can wound.

Not only are these wounding words the opposite of what we would want others to do to us (Matthew 7:12), they are in a certain sense violations of the fifth commandment, "Thou shalt not kill." When you let fly words of gossip, unwarranted criticism or slander, you can inflict grievous injury to another's reputation (and, it goes without saying, to their feelings), even to the point of character assassination—murdering that person's good name through your words.

This is why the Bible warns us against these sins. Ponder these passages and ask yourself and the Lord if you don't have some repair work to do for failing in charity towards your neighbor (or wife, husband, child, relative, coworker, friend or enemy).

Ecclesiastes 7:21 "Do not give heed to all the things that men say, lest you hear your servant cursing you; your heart knows that many times you have yourself cursed others."

Sirach 5:11–14 "Be quick to hear, / and be deliberate in answering. / If you have understanding, answer your neighbor; / but if not, put your hand on your mouth. / Glory and dishonor come from speaking, / and a man's tongue is his downfall. / Do not be called a slanderer, / and do not lie in ambush with your tongue; / for shame comes to the thief, / and severe condemnation to the double-tongued."

Sirach 28:15–18 "Slander has driven away courageous women, / and deprived them of the fruit of their toil. / Whoever pays heed to slander will not find rest, / nor will he settle down in peace. / The blow of a whip raises a welt, / but a blow of the tongue crushes the bones. / Many have fallen by the edge of the sword, / but not so many as have fallen because of the tongue."

Psalm 15:1–3 "O LORD, who shall sojourn in thy tent? / Who shall dwell on thy holy hill? / He who walks blamelessly, and does what is right, / and speaks truth from his heart; / who does not slander with his tongue, / and does no evil to his friend, / nor takes up a reproach against his neighbor."

Matthew 5:21–22 "You have heard that it was said to the men of old, 'You shall not kill; and whoever kills shall be liable to judgment.' But I say to you that every one who is angry with his brother shall be liable to judgment; whoever insults his brother shall be liable to the council, and whoever says, 'You fool!' shall be liable to the hell of fire."

Matthew 15:17–20 "Do you not see that whatever goes into the mouth passes into the stomach, and so passes on? But what comes out of the mouth proceeds from the heart, and this defiles a man.

For out of the heart come evil thoughts, murder, adultery, fornication, theft, false witness, slander. These are what defile a man."

James 4:11–12 "Do not speak evil against one another, brethren. He that speaks evil against a brother or judges his brother, speaks evil against the law and judges the law. But if you judge the law, you are not a doer of the law but a judge. There is one lawgiver and judge, he who is able to save and to destroy. But who are you that you judge your neighbor?"

And finally, we do well to keep in mind the Lord's warning about the power that our words have, for good and for evil, and what will await us as recompense for those words: "I tell you, on the day of judgment men will render account for every careless word they utter; for by your words you will be justified, and by your words you will be condemned" (Matthew 12:36–37).

Further Reading: Psalm 35:19–22 ; Proverbs 10:16–20;
Matthew 22:37–39; Luke 12:2–3; Romans 1:26–32;
Colossians 3:5–10; Ephesians 4:30; 1 Timothy 3:1–9;
1 Peter 2:1–3
CCC, 2465–2492

8

Is Drinking Alcohol a Sin?

Comedian Henny Youngman once quipped, "When I read about the evils of drinking, I gave up reading." His wisecrack reveals something about how people approach the question of whether or not drinking alcohol is a sin.

For some, including many evangelical Protestants, Scripture's prohibitions against drunkenness are enough to convince them that drinking alcohol is itself forbidden. Others who enjoy getting drunk simply ignore the Bible's warnings, imagining either that drunkenness isn't really a big deal or that those warnings don't apply to them.

Well, what the Bible actually says on this issue may surprise and disappoint people in both camps.

First, let's be clear that intentional drunkenness is a mortal sin. (1 John 5:16–17; see also CCC 1852, 2290). Galatians 5:19–21 tells us: "Now the works of the flesh are plain: immorality, impurity, licentiousness, idolatry, sorcery, enmity, strife, jealousy, anger, selfishness, dissension, party spirit, envy, drunkenness, carousing, and the like. *I warn you, as I warned you before, that those who do such things shall not inherit the kingdom of God*" (emphasis added).

Saint Peter wrote, "Let the time that is past suffice for doing what the Gentiles like to do, living in licentiousness, passions, drunkenness, revels, carousing, and lawless idolatry. They are surprised that you do not now join them in the same wild profligacy, and they abuse you; but they will give account to him who is ready to judge the living and the dead" (1 Peter 4:3–5).

The Old Testament contains many warnings against drunkenness. Noah's wine-bender in Genesis 9:20–27 was the first of a long line of examples. Lot's experience with too much wine and the shocking sexual sins that ensued was, if you'll forgive the pun, a sobering reminder about the dangers of drunkenness.

Proverbs 20:1 says, "Wine is a mocker, strong drink a brawler; / and whoever is led astray by it is not wise."

Sirach 31:27–31 shows that getting drunk is sinful, but drinking itself is not:

> Wine is like life to men, / if you drink it in moderation. / What is life to a man who is without wine? / It has been created to make men glad. / Wine drunk in season and temperately / is rejoicing of heart and gladness of soul. / Wine drunk to excess is bitterness of soul, / with provocation and stumbling. / Drunkenness increases the anger of a fool to his injury, / reducing his strength and adding wounds.

The Lord reminds us, however, that wine and strong drink can be a good thing when used correctly. "[B]ind up the money in your hand, and go the places which the LORD your God chooses, and spend the money for whatever you desire, oxen, or sheep, or wine or strong drink, whatever your appetite craves; and you shall eat there before the LORD your God and rejoice, you and your household" (Deuteronomy 14:25–26). (Some translations render this last phrase more literally as "making merry before the Lord.")

Wine played an integral role in both the old and new covenants. In Genesis 14:17–18 the covenant between Abraham and Melchizedek was enacted with an offering of bread and wine. Christ used bread and wine at the Last Supper to transubstan-tiate into his Body and Blood (Matthew 26:26; Mark 14:22; Luke 22:19; 1 Corinthians 11:23–26).

Saint Paul didn't say, "Don't drink wine" (see Ephesians 5:18), which would have been a complete prohibition. Rather, he said, don't to drink wine to excess.

The Catholic Church teaches, as common sense testifies, that drinking wine and other forms of alcohol, like food, sex, laughter and dancing, is good when enjoyed in its proper time and context. To abuse any good thing is a sin, but the thing abused does not itself become sinful. As Saint Paul said, "'All things are lawful for me,' but not all things are helpful. 'All things are lawful for me,' but I will not be enslaved by anything" (1 Corinthians 6:12).

Some who oppose drinking argue the kind of wine Christ approved of is the kind that doesn't intoxicate. But "wine" without alcohol isn't wine at all—it's essentially grape juice.

The Lord drank wine (Luke 7:34)—often enough, apparently, that his detractors accused him of being a drunkard. His first recorded miracle was to turn water into wine (John 2:1–11). If the Lord had changed water into grape juice, why would the head waiter at the wedding at Cana have said, "Every man serves the good wine first; and when men have drunk freely, then the poor wine; but you have kept the good wine until now" (John 2:10)?

Guzzle as much grape juice as you like, and you won't get drunk. It won't impair your ability to distinguish between "poor" and "good." But drinking too much wine will.

Further Reading: Genesis 14:18; Deuteronomy 7:12–16; Ecclesiastes 10:17, 19; Sirach 31:12–30; Tobit 4:14–15; Psalm 104:15; Proverbs 23:21; Habakkuk 2:15; Isaiah 5:11; Luke 21:34–36; Romans 13:12–14; 1 Timothy 5:23
CCC, 1801, 1852, 1866, 2290

9

Humility

In *The Gulag Archipelago* Aleksandr Solzhenitsyn wrote, "Pride grows in the human heart like lard on a pig."[1]

Since all of us suffer in varying degrees from the ill effects of pride, we would do well to go on a spiritual diet and trim away some of the lard. Happily, the Lord has created a fast-acting secret ingredient to help us shed our pride. We call it humility. It's the virtue that corrects this vice and Sacred Scripture contains a lot of information on how, with God's grace, we can grow in humility and conquer our pride.

The word "humility" derives from the Latin word for dirt, *humus*. This tells us something about the quality of lowliness inherent in humility for what could be more lowly than the ground beneath one's feet?

Humility is the virtue by which we acknowledge our own limitations and imperfections knowing that God, our loving Father, is the Creator and Author of all life. It allows us to freely submit ourselves to him without pride and in willing service to others.

We can see the first reminder of man's need for humility in God's words to Adam and Eve in Genesis 3:19, "In the sweat of your face / you shall eat bread / till you return to the ground, / for out of it you were taken: / you are dust, / and to dust you shall return." Every Ash Wednesday, the priest who traces the sign of the cross on your forehead with ashes repeats this ancient reminder. The ashes signify both the humility of repentance and penance (i.e., wearing sackcloth and ashes, cf. Isaiah 58:5, Daniel 9:3, Luke 10:13) as well as the fact that we will all, eventually, die and our bodies will return for a time to the lowly *humus* from which we were brought forth in Adam and Eve.

Here are just a few of the many Scriptural teachings on the beauty and importance of the virtue of humility:

Matthew 5:5 "Blessed are the meek, for they shall inherit the earth."

Matthew 11:29 "[Christ said,] Take my yoke upon you, and learn from me; for I am gentle and lowly in heart, and you will find rest for your souls."

1 Peter 5:5 "Clothe yourselves, all of you, with humility toward one another, for 'God opposes the proud, but gives grace to the humble.'"

Matthew 8:8 "[T]he centurion answered him, 'Lord, I am not worthy to have you come under my roof; but only say the word, and my servant will be healed.'"

Zephaniah 2:3 "Seek the LORD, all you humble of the land, / who do his commands; / seek righteousness, seek humility; / perhaps you may be hidden / on the day of the wrath of the LORD."

Psalm 149:4 "For the LORD takes pleasure in his people; / he adorns the humble with victory."

Proverbs 11:2 "When pride comes, then comes disgrace; / but with the humble is wisdom" (see also Proverbs 3:4).

Isaiah 57:15 "For thus says the high and lofty One /who inhabits eternity, whose name is Holy: / 'I dwell in the high and holy place, / and also with him who is of a contrite and humble spirit,

/ to revive the spirit of the humble, / and to revive the heart of the contrite.'"

Philippians 2:3–4 "Do nothing from selfishness or conceit, but in humility count others better than yourselves. Let each of you look not only to his own interests, but also to the interests of others."

Colossians 3:12 "Put on then, as God's chosen ones, holy and beloved, compassion, kindness, lowliness, meekness, and patience...."

James 4:6, 10 "'God opposes the proud, but gives grace to the humble.'... [therefore] Humble yourselves before the Lord and he will exalt you."

Matthew 20:25–28 "But Jesus called them to him and said, 'You know that the rulers of the Gentiles lord it over them, and their great men exercise authority over them. It shall not be so among you; but whoever would be great among you must be your servant, and whoever would be first among you must be your slave; even as the Son of man came not to be served but to serve, and to give his life as a ransom for many.'"

Matthew 23:11–12 "He who is greatest among you shall be your servant; whoever exalts himself will be humbled, and whoever humbles himself will be exalted."

John 13:3–9, 12–15 "Jesus, knowing that the Father had given all things into his hands, and that he had come from God and was going to God, rose from supper, laid aside his garments, and girded himself with a towel. Then he poured water into a basin, and began to wash the disciples' feet, and to wipe them with the towel with which he was girded. He came to Simon Peter; and Peter said to him, 'Lord, do you wash my feet?' Jesus answered him, 'What I am doing you do not know now, but afterward you will understand.' Peter said to him, 'You shall never wash my feet.'

Jesus answered him, 'If I do not wash you, you have no part in me.' Simon Peter said to him, 'Lord, not my feet only but also my hands and my head!'… When he had washed their feet, and taken his garments, and resumed his place, he said to them, 'Do you know what I have done to you? You call me Teacher and Lord; and you are right, for so I am. If I then, your Lord and Teacher, have washed your feet, you also ought to wash one another's feet. For I have given you an example, that you also should do as I have done to you.'"

1 Corinthians 1:26–31   "For consider your call, brethren; not many of you were wise according to worldly standards, not many were powerful, not many were of noble birth; but God chose what is foolish in the world to shame the wise, God chose what is weak in the world to shame the strong, God chose what is low and despised in the world, even things that are not, to bring to nothing things that are, so that no human being might boast in the presence of God. He is the source of your life in Christ Jesus, whom God made our wisdom, our righteousness and sanctification and redemption."

One final verse to ponder is Luke 18:13, which contains one of the most simple, heartfelt and humble statements of trust in the Lord: "God, be merciful to me a sinner!"

Further Reading: Proverbs 22:4; Sirach 10:7–19; Luke 1:46–53; Ephesians 4:1–2

10

Homosexuality

These days, the issue of homosexuality is constantly present in the media and in our culture. As a result, many now hold the view that homosexual activity is just as acceptable and natural as heterosexual activity. But in spite of those Catholics who commit homosexual sins, the Church remains steadfast in her teaching: "You shall not lie with a male as with a woman; it is an abomination" (Leviticus 18:22).

While affirming the human dignity of homosexuals as men and women whom God loves and has made in his image, the Church also affirms the reality that deliberate homosexual activity is gravely sinful. Homosexuality involves a violation of natural law. When we violate God's laws, we violate our very humanity by misusing the faculties with which he entrusted us, such as our sexuality and procreative abilities.

The *Catechism* explains:

> Homosexuality refers to relations between men or between women who experience an exclusive or predominant sexual attraction toward persons of the same sex. It has taken a great variety of forms through the centuries and in different cultures. Its psychological genesis remains largely unexplained. Basing itself on Sacred Scripture, which presents homosexual acts as acts of grave depravity, [cf. *Gen* 19:1-29;

Rom 1:24-27; *1 Cor* 6:10; *1 Tim* 1:10] tradition has always declared that "homosexual acts are intrinsically disordered" [CDF, *Persona humana* 8]. They are contrary to the natural law. They close the sexual act to the gift of life. They do not proceed from a genuine affective and sexual complementarity. Under no circumstances can they be approved. (CCC, 2357)[1]

In the Old Covenant, homosexual activity was punishable by death. "If a man lies with a male as with a woman, both of them have committed an abomination; they shall be put to death, their blood is upon them" (Leviticus 20:13). Thankfully, in the New Covenant that punishment no longer applies, but the Church reminds us of an even *worse* eternal punishment that awaits those (whether homosexual or heterosexual) who refuse to repent and turn from their sins.

We know that the judgment of God rightly falls upon those who do such things. Do you suppose, O man, that when you judge those who do such things and yet do them yourself, you will escape the judgment of God? Or do you presume upon the riches of his kindness and forbearance and patience? Do you not know that God's kindness is meant to lead you to repentance? But by your hard and impenitent heart you are storing up wrath for yourself on the day of wrath when God's righteous judgment will be revealed. For he will render to every man according to his works: to those who by patience in well-doing seek for glory and honor and immortality, he will give eternal life; but for those who are factious and do not obey the truth, but obey wickedness, there will be wrath and fury. (Romans 2:2–8)

Saint Paul warned: "For this reason God gave them up to dishonorable passions. Their women exchanged natural relations for unnatural, and the men likewise gave up natural relations with women and were consumed with passion for one another, men committing shameless acts with men and receiving in their own persons the due penalty for their error" (Romans 1:26–27; see 1:18–22).

Saint Peter wrote:

> God did not spare the angels when they sinned, but cast them into hell and committed them to pits of nether gloom to be kept until the judgment…he did not spare the ancient world, but preserved Noah, a herald of righteousness, with seven other persons, when he brought a flood upon the world of the ungodly…by turning the cities of Sodom and Gomorrah to ashes he condemned them to extinction and made them an example to those who were to be ungodly (2 Peter 2:4–6).

Some proponents of homosexuality try to twist the meaning of the account of the homosexual sins of Sodom and Gomorrah in Genesis 19:1–14. In this famous episode, a righteous man named Lot shielded two men (actually angels) who were guests in his home from some townsmen who sought to rape them. Some will argue that God punished Sodom and Gomorrah not for the sin of homosexuality but for "not showing hospitality."

This argument is bogus. Read Genesis 19 carefully, and notice that Lot, an inhabitant of that city, indeed showed hospitality to these strangers. He protected them from the mob of men who wanted to homosexually rape them. A lack of hospitality has nothing to do with what happened. And you won't find any examples of the Lord destroying a city with fire and brimstone just because folks didn't roll out the welcome mat to strangers.

Further Reading: Leviticus 18:19–30; Deuteronomy 23:17; Judges 19:14–29; 1 Kings 14:24; 15:12; 22:46; 2 Kings 23:7; Matthew 19:4–5; 1 Corinthians 6:9–10; 1 Timothy 1:9–10; 2 Peter 2:7–10; Jude 1:7
CCC, 1950–1958, 1975–1976, 2331–2379

11

Why Do Catholics Worship on Sunday and Not on the Sabbath?

Christians have worshiped on Sunday instead of on the Sabbath since the days of the Apostles. But the practice of observing the Lord's Day (that is, Sunday) instead of the Sabbath seems to some to be contrary to the Ten Commandments.

Groups such as the Seventh-Day Adventists object to Sunday worship as being a violation of God's commands. They criticize the Catholic Church for "changing" one of God's eternal decrees. Let's examine the scriptural evidence to see what conclusions we should draw.

First, note in Exodus 20:8–10 that the Lord God said to Moses, "Remember the sabbath day, to keep it holy. Six days you shall labor, and do all your work; but the seventh day is a sabbath to the LORD your God; in it you shall not do any work." This commandment was a "perpetual covenant" that God wanted his people to observe through the ages (Exodus 31:16–18; Deuteronomy 5:12). Henceforth, the Jews have observed the Sabbath on Saturday, resting from all work and emulating God's own rest on the seventh day of creation (Genesis 2:1–3).

The Catholic Church did not abandon this commandment, as some erroneously claim. Rather, observance of the third commandment to "keep holy the Sabbath" was *transferred* to Sunday, also known as "The Lord's Day" (Acts 20:7; 1 Corinthians 16:2), because it is through his resurrection that we become a "new creation" (2 Corinthians 5:17; Galatians 6:15).

Around the year AD 100, the *Didache* instructed Christians to "gather together on the Lord's Day." In AD 155 Saint Justin Martyr wrote a letter to the Roman emperor mentioning that the early Church celebrated the eucharistic liturgy on Sundays instead of Saturday. This practice was already universal.

The early Church transferred the observance of the third commandment from Saturday to Sunday for two primary reasons: First, Sunday is the day Christ rose from the dead (Matthew 28:1; John 20:1), and as Saint Paul said, if Christ did *not* rise from the dead, we are the most pitiable of people because our faith is in vain.

Second, the early Christians sought to differentiate themselves from Judaism. This included their abandonment of Judaism's system of ritual animal sacrifices. Christ is the Lamb of God who takes away the sins of the world (John 1:29, 36), and his perfect sacrifice replaced the old covenant Passover lamb, which was ritually slain and consumed as mere symbol of sacrifice for sin. Similarly, Christians relinquished other Jewish ceremonial rituals and precepts, such as the kosher food laws and dietary restrictions imposed by the law of Moses (Deuteronomy 12:15–28; 14:3–21) and the observance of the Passover and other Jewish feast days (Colossians 2:16–23).

The early Christians wanted to show forth the true meaning of the Sabbath, which achieved its full purpose in the new covenant of Christ, in whom we find our perfect, ultimate rest. "Come to me, all who labor and are heavy laden, and I will give you rest" (Matthew 11:28).

The old covenant Sabbath, temple ceremonies and animal sacrifices prefigured in an imperfect way Christ's perfect fulfillment in and through the new covenant. The Old Covenant observances were but "a copy and shadow of the heavenly sanctuary" (Hebrews 8:5; see 10:1). Once the perfect had come, the imperfect passed away. Just as baptism replaced the old covenant ordinance of circumcision, the Church came to observe the third commandment in a new way.

As Saint Paul wrote, "Therefore let no one pass judgment on you in questions of food and drink or with regard to a festival or a new moon or a sabbath. These are only a shadow of what is to come; but the substance belongs to Christ" (Colossians 2:16–17). And in Galatians 4:9–11 he scolds Christians who still clung to the old covenant restrictions and ceremonies. The ritual observance of the Sabbath was part of the old covenant. But in Christ, we are no longer bound by the old covenant. So the demands and obligations of the old covenant, including the ritual observance of the Sabbath, have passed away, having been replaced by the spiritual observance of the Sabbath in the new covenant.

Interestingly, in Matthew 19:16–22, when the rich young man asked what one must do to be saved, Christ enumerated several of the Ten Commandments. He did not mention the third commandment: keeping holy the Sabbath.

Seventh-Day Adventists argue that the Catholic Church had no authority to change the third commandment. But the fact is that Christ established the Catholic Church and granted it the authority to "bind and loose" (Matthew 18:18) and to teach with his own authority (Luke 10:16, Matthew 28:18–20). Now, since Christ revealed that he is the Lord even of the Sabbath Day (Matthew 12:8; Mark 2:28; Luke 6:5) and that the Sabbath was "made for man, not man for the Sabbath" (Mark 2:27), it follows that his Church also has a share in that authority (Matthew 10:40).

As Christ said to Simon Peter, "I will give you the keys of the kingdom of heaven, and *whatever you bind on earth shall be bound in heaven, and whatever you loose on earth shall be loosed in heaven"* (Matthew 16:19, emphasis added; see 18:18–20).

Notice also that the Seventh-Day Adventists themselves do not observe the "eternal commandment" of circumcision given by God to Abraham in Genesis 17. This commandment predated by hundreds of years the Ten Commandments given to Moses, and holds no less weight. And yet, as even Seventh-Day Adventists are forced to admit (since they do not practice ritual circumcision), the Bible does not show that Jesus Christ expressly taught that God's commandment regarding circumcision was to be changed to the sacrament of baptism. The Church had the authority— Christ's authority—to enact that change. In so doing, it did not abandon God's eternal commandment regarding circumcision, but instead observed that commandment in a new and perfected form, that of the sacrament of baptism (Galatians 3:27–29; Colossians 2:11–12).

This is a helpful parallel with the Church's authority to transfer the observance of the Sabbath from Saturday to Sunday. It was not an abandonment of God's law but rather a fulfillment and a perfecting of that law. As Christ explained, "Think not that I have come to abolish the law and the prophets; I have come not to abolish them but to fulfil them. For truly, I say to you, till heaven and earth pass away, not an iota, not a dot, will pass from the law until all is accomplished" (Matthew 5:17–18).

Further Reading: Luke 10:16; Acts 15; 20:7; 2 Corinthians 5:1–5; Galatians 5:2; Colossians 2:16–17
CCC, 128–130, 2175, 2168–2195

12

Profanity, Blasphemy and Purity of Speech

In the summer of 1975, Frankie Valli's hit single "Swearin' to God" came out and climbed the charts. As you'd expect, millions of radio listeners sang along. The problem is that this song was a clear if seemingly benign example of taking the Lord's name in vain—something God commanded us not to do: "You shall not take the name of the LORD your God in vain; for the LORD will not hold him guiltless who takes his name in vain" (Exodus 20:7; see Deuteronomy 5:11).

But beyond sappy song lyrics lies the larger problem of what in former days was known as "impure speech"—the use of profanity and blasphemy. And it's a widespread failing. Many people imagine that the way they speak is of no lasting importance in God's eyes, but they are sadly mistaken.

We can divide the problem of impure speech into two categories: *profanity*, which is the use of crude swear words, and *blasphemy*, which is the use of swear words in combination with God's name.

The *Catechism* explains that blasphemy offends against the second commandment by expressing, in thoughts or words, any form of contempt or mockery toward God, the Blessed Virgin Mary, the saints, the Church, the sacraments, sacred images, or other sacred things. Because the Lord is all holy, any intentional insult to him or his name is a mortal sin (see CCC, 2148, 2150). Scripture condemns those who blaspheme the name of Jesus by which we are called to the Father (James 2:7).

In the Old Testament, blaspheming God, even just by using his name in vain in casual conversation, was punishable by death (Leviticus 24:15–16).

The Bible is clear that it is not acceptable for Christians (indeed, for anyone) to use profanity. We should strive to be pure in thought, word and deed, both because profanity and blasphemy offend God and can be a mortal sin, and because such speech is the sure sign of a spiritually (not to mention socially) immature person. True spiritual maturity leaves no room for crude and blasphemous language.

Saint Paul taught us that "whatever is true, whatever is honorable, whatever is just, whatever is pure, whatever is lovely, whatever is gracious, if there is any excellence, if there is anything worthy of praise, think about these things" (Philippians 4:8). And Christ pointed to our need for pure speech when he exhorted us to "be perfect, as your heavenly Father is perfect" (Matthew 5:48).

Consider these other scriptural warnings on this theme:

Mark 7:20–23 "What comes out of a man is what defiles a man. For from within, out of the heart of man, come evil thoughts, fornication, theft, murder, adultery, coveting, wickedness, deceit, licentiousness, envy, slander, pride, foolishness. All these evil things come from within, and they defile a man."

Isaiah 6:5–7 "And I said: 'Woe is me! For I am lost; for I am a man of unclean lips, and I dwell in the midst of a people of unclean lips; for my eyes have seen the King, the LORD of hosts!'

Then flew one of the seraphim to me, having in his hand a burning coal which he had taken with tongs from the altar. And he touched my mouth, and said: 'Behold, this has touched your lips; your guilt is taken away, and your sin forgiven.'"

Sirach 27:11–14 "The talk of the godly man is always wise, / but the fool changes like the moon. / Among stupid people watch for a chance to leave, / but among thoughtful people stay on. / The talk of fools is offensive, / and their laughter is wantonly sinful. / The talk of men given to swearing makes one's hair stand on end, / and their quarrels make a man stop his ears."

James 3:6–12 "And the tongue is a fire. The tongue is an unrighteous world among our members, staining the whole body, setting on fire the cycle of nature, and set on fire by hell. For every kind of beast and bird, of reptile and sea creature, can be tamed and has been tamed by humankind, but no human being can tame the tongue—a restless evil, full of deadly poison. With it we bless the Lord and Father, and with it we curse men, who are made in the likeness of God. From the same mouth come blessing and cursing. My brethren, this ought not to be so."

Colossians 4:6 "Let your speech always be gracious, seasoned with salt, so that you may know how you ought to answer every one."

If you have a problem with profanity or blasphemy (or both), repent to the Lord with sincere contrition, go to sacramental confession, and firmly commit to rely on God's loving grace to help you avoid this sin in the future. It may not be easy at first, but in time and with God's help you can unlearn that bad habit. And just think, besides being a more enjoyable person to be around, the payoff for you will be eternal. Remember what Christ said: "Blessed are the pure in heart, for they shall see God" (Matthew 5:8). The converse is also true: Those who are not pure in heart shall not see God.

Which group will you be in?

Further Reading: Psalm 59; 109:17–18; Hosea 4:1–3;
Matthew 15:19–20; Mark 7:21–23; 1 Corinthians 6:12–20;
1 Thessalonians 4:1–10; 1 Timothy 4:11; Titus 2:8;
Revelation 21:27

13

Why Confess to a Priest?

Why should I confess my sins to a *priest?*" the young woman at the microphone demanded of me. "As a Christian, I confess my sins directly to *God.*" Her question, raised at one of my recent parish apologetics seminars, is common among Protestants.

While there is no explicit statement in Scripture that says, "Confess your sins to a priest," there is a wealth of implicit evidence that leads to this conclusion.

Remember, it's not an "either-or" proposition—either one confesses his sins directly to God, or he confesses them to a priest. Rather, it's a "both-and" situation—no Catholic can make a good sacramental confession without first confessing directly to God. Only then can one properly receive the sacrament of confession, receiving sacramental absolution from the priest, who ministers *in persona Christi* (in the Person of Christ) (Luke 10:16; 2 Corinthians 5:18–20).

Ultimately, God alone can forgive sins (Mark 2:7). Christ, who is God, possesses this authority (Matthew 9:5–8; Mark 2:8–11), which he conferred in a subordinate way upon his Apostles when he said, "'As the Father has sent me, even so I send you.' And when he had said this, he breathed on them, and said to them, 'Receive the Holy Spirit. If you forgive the sins of any, they are forgiven; if you retain the sins of any, they are retained'" (John 20:22–23).

The special authority was not merely to declare sins to be forgiven, but to actually *forgive* them, in the name of Christ.

Second Corinthians 5:18–20 says,

> All this is from God, who through Christ reconciled us to himself and gave us the ministry of reconciliation; that is, God was in Christ reconciling the world to himself, not counting their trespasses against them, and entrusting to us the message of reconciliation. So we are ambassadors for Christ, God making his appeal through us. We beseech you on behalf of Christ, be reconciled to God.

Notice that Saint Paul says this ministry was entrusted to "us," and that "we" are ministers of reconciliation, and that God is appealing through "us." Then he switches to "you," saying "we beseech you to be reconciled to God." This indicates that Saint Paul was speaking about two distinct groups here: those who are ministers of reconciliation, and those who are reconciled to God through their ministry.

This priestly ministry of forgiving sins is linked to Christ's promise: "He who hears you hears me, and he who rejects you rejects me" (Luke 10:16; see Matthew 10:40); and "[W]hatever you bind on earth shall be bound in heaven, and whatever you loose on earth shall be loosed in heaven" (Matthew 18:18).

James 5:14–16 says, "Is any among you sick? Let him call for the elders of the Church, and let them pray over him, anointing him with oil in the name of the Lord; and the prayer of faith will save the sick man, and the Lord will raise him up; and if he has committed sins, he will be forgiven. Therefore confess your sins to one another, and pray for one another, that you may be healed." This passage links the forgiveness of sins with the prayers and ministry of the priests [i.e., elders, presbyters] and with the act of confessing one's sins. And while the phrase "confess your sins to one another" could reasonably be understood to refer to Christians ingeneral, the emphasis on the ministry of the priests here offers an implicit indication of their unique role in forgiving sins.

Mark 1:40–44 tells about a leper who approached Christ and asked to be healed of his illness:

> And a leper came to him beseeching him,… "If you wish, you can make me clean." Moved with pity, he stretched out his hand and touched him, and said to him, "I will; be clean." And immediately the leprosy left him, and he was made clean. And he sternly charged him, and sent him away at once, and said to him, "See that you say nothing to any one; but go, show yourself to the priest, and offer for your cleansing what Moses commanded, for a proof to the people." (see also Matthew 8:1–4; Luke 5:12–14).

There's a parallel between what happened to this leper and confession to a priest.

Sin, especially mortal sin, is like leprosy—a contagious and horribly disfiguring disease that causes one's flesh to literally rot away. The leper is like the sinner. He asked Christ for healing, as Catholics do by repenting and turning away from sin. Christ healed the leper just as he forgives the repentant sinner. But notice that Christ didn't simply heal the leper and send him on his way. He instructed him to go into the city and present himself to the priest so that the priest could examine him and verify the cure; upon that determination, the priest would formally declare the man to be healed and permit him to reenter society. Similarly, in the sacrament of confession, the priest absolves the penitent. He then imposes a penance on the penitent; the cured leper likewise performed a sacrifice of ritual expiation (Leviticus 14). From this passage we can see why Christ instituted the great sacrament of confession.

As 1 John 1:9 says, "*If we confess our sins,* he is faithful and just, and will forgive our sins and cleanse us from all unrighteousness" (emphasis added).

Further Reading: Leviticus 5:5; Numbers 5:5–7; Job 31:33, 40; Proverbs 28:13; Psalm 38:18; Sirach 4:26; Matthew 3:6; 16:19; 18:18; Mark 2:7; Acts 19:18; 1 John 1:9–10
CCC, 1424–1497

14

Defending the Faith

Some people are puzzled by the word "apologetics." It's not a commonly heard term, and it also seems to imply that one regrets or feels remorse for having done something wrong. To say, "I apologize" is the same as saying, "I'm sorry for what I did." But "apologetics" has exactly the opposite meaning.

The classic term for defending the faith is "apologetics." This English word derives from the Greek word *apología* and its Latin cognate *apológia*. Both mean "to give a defense" or an explanation for something. It's in this sense that we encounter apologetics in the Bible.

For example, in 1 Peter 3:15 we are told to "Always be prepared to make a defense [Greek: *apologían*] to any one who calls you to account for the hope that is in you, yet do it with gentleness and reverence." It's worth noting that this exhortation from the first pope to be ready always to do apologetics applies to all baptized Catholics, whether laymen or priests, young or old, married or single.

Saint Paul echoes this universal call to all Christians when he says in Philippians 1:7, "[Y]ou are all partakers with me of grace, both in my imprisonment and in the defense [*apología*] and confirmation of the gospel." Each of us has a role to play in defending the faith.

Philippians 1:15–16 tells us, "Some indeed preach Christ from envy and rivalry, but others from good will. The latter do it out of love, knowing that I am put here for the defense [*apologían*] of the gospel." This passage is reminiscent of the Old Testament example of engaging in apologetics purely for the benefit of the other person: "Now therefore stand still, that I may plead with you before the LORD concerning all the saving deeds of the LORD which he performed for you and for your fathers" (1 Samuel 12:7).

Saint Jude wrote, "Beloved, being very eager to write to you of our common salvation, I found it necessary to write appealing to you to contend for the faith which was once for all delivered to the saints" (Jude 3). It's interesting that Saint Jude "found it necessary" to remind those original Catholics of their obligation to stand up for the truth. It's a good reminder for us today, as there are now so many opportunities to stand up for the faith.

The key to practicing authentic Catholic apologetics—according to the mind of the Church and the example of the Apostles—is to be, above all, unswervingly charitable and patient. Authentic Catholic apologetics should never be defensive or abrasive. Properly done, it should be an *invitation*, not a provocation. Our goal is to help people come closer to Christ and the Catholic Church, not to drive them away by our obnoxious behavior.

This means, then, that our use of the tools of reason, the facts of Christian history and the proofs for the Catholic Church in Sacred Scripture must always be careful and purposeful and used for the benefit of the other person, the way a surgeon uses his instruments to correct problems in his patient and, eventually, to heal him. Our approach to apologetics should always be calm, patient and rational, modeled on God's own invitation, "Come now, let us reason together, / says the LORD" (Isaiah 1:18).

If we attempt to explain and defend the faith with a haughty or triumphalistic attitude, or if we just want to win an argument or "get back" at someone, we are doing apologetics for the wrong reason. Our efforts will almost certainly backfire, repelling the other person and likely driving him or her further away from Christ and the Church. We must never allow our ego to be involved in evangelization and apologetics.

Echoing Saint Peter's admonition to defend the faith with "gentleness and respect," Saint Paul reminds us to

> Have nothing to do with stupid, senseless controversies; you know that they breed quarrels. And the Lord's servant must not be quarrelsome but kindly to every one, an apt teacher, forbearing, correcting his opponents with gentleness. God may perhaps grant that they will repent and come to know the truth, and they may escape from the snare of the devil, after being captured by him to do his will (2 Timothy 2:23–26).

He also said, "Conduct yourselves wisely toward outsiders, making the most of the time. Let your speech always be gracious, seasoned with salt, so that you may know how you ought to answer every one" (Colossians 4:5–6).

Daniel 3:16–17 shows us that sometimes you must stand your ground and do what's right, come what may. And 2 Corinthians 12:19 reminds us that apologetics doesn't mean defending *our* teachings, but the Lord's: "Have you been thinking all along that we have been defending ourselves before you? It is in the sight of God that we have been speaking in Christ, and all for your upbuilding, beloved."

The Apostles evangelized everywhere they went (Acts 2) but sometimes had to engage specifically in apologetics to defend Christ's teachings. For example, in Acts 22:1 Saint Paul said, "Brethren and fathers, hear the defense [*apologías*] which I now

make before you." Acts 5:17–42 and 18:9–10 provide other examples of the Apostles engaging in apologetics.

You too can practice apologetics, regardless of what you do for
a living, where you live, how old or young you may be or what your
educational background is. What matters is that Christ has called
you, by virtue of your baptism, to be his Apostle to those around
you. That's right—Christ wants *you* to be his Apostle.

Listen to the words of the prophet Amos: "Then Amos
answered Amaziah, 'I am no prophet, nor a prophet's son; but I
am a herdsman, and a dresser of sycamore trees, and the LORD
took me from following the flock, and the LORD said to me, "Go,
prophesy to my people Israel"'" (Amos 7:14–16; see Acts 4:13).

Further Reading: Psalm 119:46; Matthew 10:16–22;
Luke 12:11–12; 25:16; 1 Corinthians 9:3; 2 Timothy 4:16–17

15

The Saints: "A Great Cloud of Witnesses"

Are the saints in heaven aware of what's happening here on earth? And if they are, do they care?

These questions are at the heart of the controversy separating Catholics from most Protestants on the subject of the communion of saints. The Catholic Church teaches that the blessed in heaven are not only aware of what's happening here on earth but are also eager to assist us with their prayerful intercession. Let's see what the Bible says about this.

Hebrews 11 describes the courageous faith of many Old Testament heroes, describing the persecution, asceticism and martyrdoms they endured. The first sentence of Hebrews 12 tells us the reason for this recounting: "Therefore, since we are surrounded by so great a cloud of witnesses, let us also lay aside every weight, and sin which clings so closely, and let us run with perseverance the race that is set before us, looking to Jesus the pioneer and perfecter of our faith" (Hebrews 12:1–2).

Notice the mention of "a great cloud of witnesses." This refers not only to the testimony and martyrdom of these witnesses (the Greek word for "witness" is *martus*)—it also refers to the fact that now, in heaven, they are witnesses from above. Now that it's our turn, they observe how we run the race toward our heavenly reward. Notice also that the same Greek word for "witness," *martus*, which is used here to describe those in heaven, is found in passages such as Matthew 18:15–16: "If your brother sins against you, go and tell him his fault, between you and him alone. If he listens to you, you have gained your brother. But if he does not listen, take one or two others along with you, that every word may be confirmed by the evidence of two or three witnesses" (see also Matthew 26:65; Luke 24:48; Acts 1:22; 2:32; 1 Timothy 6:12). This passage demonstrates how a "witness" is one who is keenly observant and aware of what's happening.

In Revelation 5:8 the saints in heaven offer the prayers of the "holy ones" (that is, the saints on earth; see Romans 8:27; Revelation 13:7) before the throne of God: "And when he had taken the scroll, the four living creatures and the twenty-four elders fell down before the Lamb, each holding a harp, and with golden bowls full of incense, which are the prayers of the saints; and they sang a new song...." We catch a glimpse of this scene again in Revelation 8:3–4.

Revelation 5:8 and 8:3–4 demonstrate that the saints in heaven are certainly aware of our prayers and supplications to God (1 Timothy 2:1–3), and that they're presenting those prayers to him.

In Revelation 6:9–11 the martyrs in heaven offer prayers of imprecation against their erstwhile persecutors on earth. They are quite aware of what's happening on earth:

When he opened the fifth seal, I saw under the altar the souls of those who had been slain for the word of God and for the witness they had borne; they cried out with a loud voice, "O Sovereign Lord, holy and true, how long before thou wilt judge and avenge our blood on those who dwell upon the earth?" Then they were each given a white robe and told to rest a little longer, until the number of their fellow servants and their brethren should be complete, who were to be killed as they themselves had been.

In Revelation 12:10–12 the saints in heaven praise those on earth who have conquered the devil through the blood of Christ. They cry, "[W]oe to you, O earth and sea, for the devil has come down to you in great wrath, because he knows that his time is short!" How would they be able to say these things if they didn't know what was happening on earth?

Similarly, in Revelation 19:1–8, the saints in heaven cry out in unison: "'Hallelujah! Salvation and glory and power belong to our God, for his judgments are true and just; he has judged the great harlot who corrupted the earth with her fornication, and he has avenged on her the blood of his servants.' Once more they cried, 'Hallelujah! The smoke from her [Babylon, a city on earth; see Revelation 14:8; 17:1–5] goes up for ever and ever.'" Again, how could the saints say this if they were unaware of earthly events?

The inexorable conclusion from such passages is that the saints in heaven are aware—very aware—of our circumstances here on earth.

And finally, Christ himself said that the saints and angels are aware of what transpires here on earth: "Just so, I tell you, there will be more joy in heaven over one sinner who repents than over ninety-nine righteous persons who need no repentance" (Luke 15:7; see 15:10). In Luke 20:36 Christ tells us that the saints in heaven are "equal to the angels."

The Bible is also clear that we can honor the saints, who shine with God's own glory as the moon reflects the light of the sun. Christ makes it clear that he gives glory to those who love him. Consider these passages:

John 17:20, 22 "I do not pray for these only, but also for those who believe in me through their word.... *The glory which thou hast* *given me I have given to them"* (emphasis added).

Romans 2:6, 10 "[God] will *render…glory and honor and peace* for every one who does good" (emphasis added).

Romans 13:7 "[Give] *honor to whom honor is due"* (emphasis added).

But are Mary and the saints aware of our prayers? Yes. Let's say that at any given moment, one million people (a tiny fraction of the world's total population of over six billion) are repenting of their sins. Christ says that the saints in heaven are somehow aware of each individual repentance. How can this be? Neither the Bible nor Sacred Tradition tells us how, but we do know, on the authority of Christ himself, that this is so.

Mary and the saints truly are a great cloud of witnesses—praying for us, encouraging us, cheering us on. When we finally cross that heavenly finish line and fall happily into their arms, we will discover just how powerful their assistance on our behalf has really been.

Further Reading: CCC, 946–962, 2683–2684

16

Does "Word of God" Always Mean "The Bible"?

It never fails. In conversations about biblical authority with evangelical and fundamentalist Protestants, this argument always comes up. The mistake here is in imagining that every time the phrase "Word of God" appears in Scripture, it refers to the *Bible*. The fact is, by paying attention to the context of the passage, we can see that most of the time the phrase "Word of God" does not refer to Scripture but to something else, such as Christ, the law, God's creative utterances or apostolic and prophetic preaching. Here are some verses that prove this:

Isaiah 55:10–11 "For as the rain and the snow come down from heaven, / and return not thither but water the earth, / making it bring forth and sprout, / giving seed to the sower and bread to the eater, / so shall my word be that goes forth from my mouth; / it shall not return to me empty, / but it shall accomplish that which I purpose, / and prosper in the thing for which I sent it." Here, the "Word of God" refers not to Scripture, but rather to God's creative word.

Luke 3:2–3 "[T]he word of God came to John the son of Zechariah in the wilderness; and he went into all the region about the Jordan, preaching a baptism of repentance." Here the phrase refers to the inspiration Saint John the Baptist received as he was sent forth to preach the gospel of repentance in preparation for Christ.

Luke 8:11–15 "Now the parable is this: The seed is the word of God. The ones along the path are those who have heard.... [T]he ones on the rock are those who, when they hear the word, receive it with joy; but these have no root, they believe for a while and in time of temptation fall away.... And as for that in the good soil, they are those who, hearing the word, hold it fast in an honest and good heart, and bring forth fruit with patience" (see Luke 4:44–5:1).

Notice the emphasis on *hearing* the Word of God—an obvious reference both to Christ's preaching and to apostolic preaching (1 Thessalonians 2:13), as well as to the continual preaching of the gospel by the Catholic Church to all creatures in all ages (Matthew 28:19–20; Romans 10:14–15).

John 1:1, 14 "In the beginning was the Word, and the Word was with God, and the Word was God.... And the Word became flesh and dwelt among us." This passage refers to the Incarnate Christ, not Scripture.

Acts 4:31 "And when they had prayed, the place in which they were gathered together was shaken; and they were all filled with the Holy Spirit and spoke the word of God with boldness."

1 Thessalonians 2:13 "[W]hen you received the word of God which you heard from us, you accepted it not as the word of men but as what it really is, the word of God, which is at work in you believers." Here Paul specifically points to oral Tradition, not to Scripture. This was his first epistle to the Thessalonians. Notice that he doesn't enjoin them to go solely by what is written in

Scripture, but reminds them to adhere to the oral teachings he had handed on to them.

Hebrews 4:12–13   "For the word of God is living and active, sharper than any two-edged sword, piercing to the division of soul and spirit, of joints and marrow, and discerning the thoughts and intentions of the heart. And before him no creature is hidden, but all are open and laid bare to the eyes of him with whom we have to do."

Protestants frequently quote passages out of context and interpret them as referring to Scripture. But notice that it speaks of the Word of God as a "him," not an "it"—it is before "him" (Christ) that the secrets of our hearts are laid bare and judged. The next time someone quotes this verse out of context, ask him to explain how it is that the Bible can "discern the thoughts and intentions of the heart." Then ask if it isn't nonsensical to think of this as Scripture, and conversely, if it's not eminently reasonable, and even demanded by the context, that one sees "Word of God" here as referring to Christ.

Hebrews 11:3 "By faith we understand that the world was created by the word of God, so that what is seen was made out of things which do not appear." This passage in Hebrews only reinforces the conclusion we draw from Hebrews 4:12–13 that the Word being spoken of there is not the Bible. Clearly, no Protestant will posit that "the world was created" by the Bible. If he does, head for the door, quickly!

17

The Blessed Trinity

Door-to-door missionaries such as Jehovah's Witnesses and Mormons will attempt to convince any Catholic who will listen that the Catholic doctrine of the Trinity is wrong. They argue that the concept of one God in three co-equal, co-eternal, consubstantial Persons is not biblical. The Bible, however, says otherwise. Based on these few representative chapters, we can see that:

+ There is only one God (Deuteronomy 6:4; Mark 12:29; 1 Timothy 2:5)

+ The Father is God (Deuteronomy 32:6; Colossians 1:2; Matthew 25:34; Luke 11:2; 1 Corinthians 15:24; Ephesians 4:6; 1 Thessalonians 1:1; John 20:17; Romans 1:7)

+ The Son, Jesus Christ, is God (John 1:1–14; 8:58; 20:28; Acts 20:28)

+ The Holy Spirit is God (John 14:16–17, 26; 16:7–14; Acts 5:3–4; 13:2–4; 21:10–11)

From these explicit truths, and under the guidance of the Holy Spirit, who guides the Church "into all truth" (John 16:12–13; see 14:25–26), the Catholic Church teaches that if there is only one God, and if the Father, Son and Holy Spirit are each God, then the doctrine of the Trinity—one God in three Persons—must also be true. Otherwise, these revelations become a jumbled mass of irreconcilable contradictions. And though one will not find the word "Trinity" in Scripture, the above passages point us toward the doctrine, which God revealed gradually, indirectly and in various ways (Hebrews 10:1).

Saint Theophilus of Antioch used the term "Trinity" in the year AD 180. He wrote in his *Epistle to Autolycus* (Autolycus was a pagan critic of the Catholic Church), that God, his Word and his Wisdom are a "Trinity" (Greek: *triados*). Some years later, Tertullian (AD 160–c. 250) coined the Latin term for "Trinity" (*trinitas*) in his work *On Modesty*. He wrote about the "Trinity of the One Divinity; Father, Son, and Holy Spirit."[1]

In addition to drawing upon the many biblical references to God's unity and transcendence, these early Church writers also cited Old Testament episodes known as *theophanies*—mysterious appearances of one or more Persons of the Trinity. References to these mysterious encounters (some of which are only implicit) are found in Genesis 1:26 (where God speaks of himself in the plural form); 3:22; 11:27; 18; Psalm 2:7; 109:1–3; Isaiah 7:14 (*Immanuel* means "God with us"); 9:6; 11:2 and 35:4. Other passages include Proverbs 8:22–31; Wisdom of Solomon 7:22–28; 8:3–8; Ezekiel 11:5, 36:27; Joel 2:28 and Malachi 3:1.

Two more explicit Trinitarian passages are found in Matthew 28:18–19 and John 1:1, 14. In the first passage, the Lord says: "All authority in heaven and on earth has been given to me. Go therefore and make disciples of all nations, baptizing them in the name of the Father and of the Son and of the Holy Spirit." Notice that Christ uses the singular form "name," not the plural "names," when he gives this directive. This usage implies the unity of the Three Divine Persons in the Trinity.

The second passage, John 1:1, 14, reads: "In the beginning was the Word [Christ], and the Word was *with* God and the Word *was* God.... And the Word became flesh and dwelt among us, full of grace and truth; we have beheld his glory, glory as of the only Son from the Father." Here we see that Christ is true God, the Second Person of the Trinity—a theme Saint Paul echoed when he wrote that Christ is "the *image* of the invisible God" (Colossians 1:15, emphasis added) and the "radiance of the glory of God and *the very stamp of his nature*" (Hebrews 1:3, emphasis added).

As the Catholic Church matured and grew, so did its theological vocabulary. Terms such as "Trinity" were developed as a way to express more precisely what the Church meant by God. And though the Church's understanding of her teaching deepened and developed, she did not invent new doctrines. Rather, she inferred truths with certitude from other truths. Some of these truths, such as that there is only one God, are explicitly taught in the Bible as well as Sacred Tradition. Since, in the sense described above, doctrine "develops" in the Catholic Church (though it never changes or ceases to mean what it once did), the First Council of Nicaea authoritatively defined the doctrine of the Trinity as dogma in AD 325.

These days, Jehovah's Witnesses, Mormons, Oneness Pentecostals and other religious groups try to convince people that the Catholic Church invented the doctrine of the Trinity, but that is simply false. The Catholic Church could not have invented the truth about the Trinity anymore than it could have invented the law of gravity—it has always been true, revealed by God himself.

Further Reading: Matthew 3:16ff; 11:27; Mark 12:29; Luke 10:22; John 10:30, 38; 14:9ff; 16:15; 17:10; Ephesians 4:6; 1 Timothy 2:5
CCC, 232–267

18

Are Catholic Prayers "Vain Repetition"?

In Matthew 6:7, Christ said, "And in praying do not heap up empty phrases as the Gentiles do; for they think that they will be heard for their many words." The Protestant King James version renders it this way: "But when ye pray, use not vain repetitions, as the heathen do: for they think that they shall be heard for their much speaking. Be not ye, therefore, like unto them." (see Sirach 7:10). Some Protestants understand the command to avoid "vain repetition" as a condemnation of formulaic Catholic prayers, such as the rosary. But did Christ really mean that repeating prayers, as Catholics do, is wrong?

No. And here's how we can know this for sure.

Christ condemned "*vain* repetition," but he did not condemn repetition itself. He singled out the prayers of pagans who invoked false gods (such as Zeus, Apollo, Diana and so on). Such prayers are vain because those gods don't exist. The priests of the false god Ba'al did exactly this in their contest against Elijah in 1 Kings 18:20–40. (Read the passage and see where all that vain babbling got them!)

But Christ could not have forbidden repetitious prayers per se because in Matthew 6:9–15, immediately after forbidding vain repetition, he gave us the greatest of all prayers: the Our Father. It seems clear that he intended this prayer to be repeated for he said, when you pray, "Pray then like this" (v. 9).

During his Passion, while in the garden of Gethsemane, Christ repeated the same prayer three times during his agony. "And going a little farther he fell on his face and prayed, 'My Father, if it be possible, let this cup pass from me; nevertheless, not as I will, but as thou wilt'…. Again, for the second time, he went away and prayed, 'My Father, if this cannot pass unless I drink it, thy will be done'…. So, leaving them again, he went away and prayed for the third time, saying the same words" (Matthew 26:39–44). Why would Christ do something that he told us was wrong, if repeating prayers was, in fact, wrong?

The Holy Spirit inspired many repetitious prayers in Scripture, intending that they be prayed and sung frequently by believers. Consider, for example, Psalm 136, which repeats the phrase "for his steadfast love [mercy] endures forever" over a dozen times! Similarly, Psalm 150 contains eleven repetitions of the prayer "praise the Lord" and "praise him" within just five verses. Daniel 3:35–68 contains many repetitions of the prayer "Bless the Lord."

And finally, look at Revelation 4:8–11: "And the four living creatures…day and night they never cease to sing, / 'Holy, holy, holy, is the Lord God Almighty, / who was and is and is to come.' / And whenever the living creatures give glory and honor and thanks to him who is seated on the throne, who lives for ever and ever." Isaiah 6:1–3 indicates that the angels in heaven also repeat this prayer continually before the throne of God.

Christ did not mean that we should not use repetitious prayers—after all, he did, the Bible does and the saints and angels in heaven do. The Bible is clear that while here on earth, we should also. Keep in mind that Christ forbade only mindless, mechanical prayers, in particular those of the pagans invoking the assistance of gods who did not even exist, much less hear and answer those prayers.

Further Reading: Ephesians 6:18; Colossians 1:9;
1 Thessalonians 3:10; 5:17; 2 Timothy 1:3
CCC, 2759–2865

19

Do Christians Have an *Absolute* Assurance of Salvation?

Many Protestants understand being "saved" as a once-in-a-lifetime moment—an act of repentance and acceptance of Jesus Christ as one's "personal Lord and savior" (a phrase that appears nowhere in the Bible, by the way). This irrevocable step eliminates the penalties of past sins, and it guarantees, no matter what might happen from that point forward, that nothing can undo or rescind one's salvation. In a life-changing moment of transformation, the lost sinner has become a saved child of God.

"Once saved always saved" is a slogan many Protestants use to describe their belief in a Christian's absolute assurance of salvation. And though not all Protestants accept the once-saved-always-saved formula, many do (Southern Baptists and the myriad of "non-denominational" denominations, for example). Two Bible passages commonly cited in support of this view are:

1 John 5:13 "I write this to you who believe in the name of the Son of God, that you may know that you have eternal life."

John 10:27–29 "My sheep hear my voice, and I know them, and they follow me; and I give them eternal life, and they shall never perish, and no one shall snatch them out of my hand. My

Father, who has given them to me, is greater than all, and no one is able to snatch them out of the Father's hand."

Saint John's assurance that "you *have* eternal life" is a proclamation of every Christian's *moral* (not absolute) assurance of salvation. Christ offers us the gift of salvation, and he will not go back on his word. But you and I are entirely capable of going back on *our* word by abandoning Christ and thereby forfeiting his gift of salvation.

Saint Paul speaks about this in 2 Timothy 2:11–13: "If we have died with him, we shall also live with him; / if we endure, we shall also reign with him; / if we deny him, he also will deny us; / if we are faithless, he remains faithful— / for he cannot deny himself."

Yes, it's true that we "have" salvation, but whether or not we keep our grasp on it is another matter, as we will see Saint Paul demonstrate in a moment.

But first, let's consider Saint John's other statement: No one can snatch out of Christ's hand those whom the Father has given him. No external power is capable of wresting us out of Christ's loving embrace (Romans 8:28–29); but *you* can do it, if you decide to willfully rebel against God through mortal sin (1 John 5:16–17).

If you die unrepentant in that state, you will have lost your salvation because you will have, in effect, snatched *yourself* out of Christ's hand. This is demonstrated by the following verses:

Romans 11:20–22 "They [i.e., those who lost their salvation by rejecting Christ] were broken off because of their unbelief, but you stand fast only through faith. So do not become proud, but stand in awe. For if God did not spare the natural branches, neither will he spare you. Note then the kindness and the severity of God: severity toward those who have fallen, but God's kindness to you, provided you continue in his kindness; otherwise you too will be cut off."

Hebrews 10:26–31 "For if we sin deliberately after receiving the knowledge of the truth, there no longer remains a sacrifice for sins, but a fearful prospect of judgment, and a fury of fire which will consume the adversaries.... How much worse punishment do you think will be deserved by the man who has spurned the Son of God, and profaned the blood of the covenant by which he was sanctified, and outraged the Spirit of grace? For we know him who said, 'Vengeance is mine, I will repay.' And again, 'The Lord will judge his people.' It is a fearful thing to fall into the hands of the living God."

2 Peter 2:20–21 "For if, after they have escaped the defilements of the world through the knowledge of our Lord and Savior Jesus Christ, they are again entangled in them and overpowered, the last state has become worse for them than the first. For it would have been better for them never to have known the way of righteousness than after knowing it to turn back from the holy commandment delivered to them."

Is there some way to "escape the defilements of the world" other than by being "saved"? No. So this means that some who have been saved fall back into grievous sin, thereby losing their salvation.

And recall the unforgiving servant in Matthew 18:21–35. Although the merciful king forgave him and wiped out his debt, the unforgiving servant proceeded to mistreat a fellow servant. When the king discovered this, he reinstated his debt and threw him into prison!

Christians can indeed lose their salvation by sinful rebellion against God, for as Christ promised, *"So also my heavenly Father will do to every one of you, if you do not forgive your brother from your heart"* (Matthew 18:35, emphasis added). Ask yourself: Why would Christ warn Christians about this, if there was no danger that it could happen to them?

Further Reading: Matthew 7:21–23; 10:22; John 5:29;
Romans 2:5–11; 8:24–25; 1 Corinthians 9:27; 10:12;
Hebrews 6:11; Philippians 2:12–13; 1 John 3:21–24; 4:20–21

20

Is It a Sin to Vote for Pro-Abortion Candidates?

Not since the Civil War crisis over slavery has a controversial moral issue so divided Americans and roiled society as has abortion. The deliberate killing of an unborn child through an abortion, though currently enjoying the "legitimacy" of legality in this country (slavery was also once legal), is, nonetheless, a grave evil that must be opposed.

But how, exactly, can one properly oppose something that is already permitted by law?

There are many peaceful, legal and constructive ways to oppose abortion and work for the overturn and elimination of the existing laws that allow for this hideous crime against children. The most direct and far-reaching method, certainly, is to vote for pro-life candidates running for political office. Or, at the very least, to *not* vote for candidates who are avowedly anti-life (that is, pro-abortion).

Regardless of political affiliations and inclinations, we should all reflect carefully on what Scripture says about how our votes will promote or prevent the continued legalization of the crime of abortion.

Let's ponder Exodus 20:13, where God commanded Moses, "Thou shalt not kill." The literal meaning of this command is "thou shalt not *murder*"—the intentional killing of an innocent life. (Someone who is guilty of a crime that is punishable by death is not being murdered when executed. [see CCC, 2261, 2263]).

Genesis 9:5–7 "For your lifeblood I will surely require a reckoning; of every beast I will require it and of man; of every man's brother I will require the life of man. Whoever sheds the blood of man, by man shall his blood be shed; for God made man in his own image. And you, be fruitful and multiply, bring forth abundantly on the earth and multiply in it." It's worth noting that in this passage the truth that humans are made in God's image is linked to the command to "be fruitful and multiply," alluding to procreation.

The unborn child is a human being made in God's image and likeness (Genesis 1:26). The unborn child is utterly innocent of having committed any evil act and, therefore, cannot under any circumstances be intentionally murdered through abortion or any other means.

And it is a fact that those who intentionally promote and perpetuate the crime of abortion through their political actions or their voting, are complicit in the sin of murder.

The Catholic Church's "Declaration on Procured Abortion" explains: "It must in any case be clearly understood that whatever may be laid down by civil law in this matter, man can never obey a law which is in itself immoral, and such is the case of a law which would admit in principle the liceity [legalization] of abortion. *Nor can he take part in a propaganda campaign in favor of such a law, or vote for it.*"[1]

Look at what God says about those who don't have the courage to stand up and speak out against this crime (and the way we vote is surely a way to do just that).

Jeremiah 7:1, 8–10 "The word that came to Jeremiah from the LORD:… 'Behold, you trust in deceptive words to no avail. Will you steal, murder, commit adultery, swear falsely, burn incense to Ba'al, and go after other gods that you have not known, and then come and stand before me in this house, which is called by my name, and say, "We are delivered!"—only to go on doing all these abominations?'" The Lord's words here apply well to Catholics today who countenance abortion and even promote it.

Wisdom of Solomon 12:1–6 "For thy immortal spirit is in all things. / Therefore thou dost correct little by little those who tres-pass, / and dost remind and warn them of the things wherein they sin, / that they may be freed from wickedness and put their trust in thee, O Lord. / Those who dwelt of old in thy holy land / thou didst hate for their detestable practices, / their works of sorcery and unholy rites, / their merciless slaughter of children, / and their sacrificial feasting on human flesh and blood. / These initi-ates from the midst of a heathen cult, / these parents who murder helpless lives, / thou didst will to destroy by the hands of our fathers."

Catholics—indeed, all Christians—have a duty before God to speak out about this great evil, to warn those who are involved in the perpetuation of legalized abortion whether by their own polit-ical actions within government or by intentionally supporting and voting for avowedly pro-abortion candidates (see Ezekiel 3:18–21).

Pro-abortion politicians and their supporters frequently attempt to cloak the objective evil of abortion with the language of righteousness and goodness, often referring to their cause as "protecting a woman's right to choose." This is simply euphemistic chicanery. It is nothing more than calling evil good.

Isaiah 5:18–21 "Woe to those who draw iniquity with cords of falsehood, / who draw sin as with cart ropes.... / Woe to those who call evil good and good evil, / who put darkness for light and light for darkness, / who put bitter for sweet and sweet for bitter! / Woe to those who are wise in their own eyes, / and shrewd in their own sight!"

When you vote in elections, consider carefully the following passage from Scripture and what it means, both for those evildoers in public office who promote abortion and for those citizens who knowingly and intentionally assist with their vote.

Isaiah 10:1–3 "Woe to those who decree iniquitous decrees, / and the writers who keep writing oppression, / to turn aside the needy from justice / and to rob the poor of my people of their right, / that widows may be their spoil, / and that they may make the fatherless their prey! / What will you do on the day of punishment, / in the storm which will come from afar? / To whom will you flee for help, / and where will you leave your wealth?"

This haunting image of those who "make the fatherless their prey" corresponds with hideous perfection to those in this country who, by promoting legalized abortion, performing abortions, and intentionally voting for pro-abortion candidates for political office, have turned the unborn child into their prey.

The aborted children who are being killed by the millions in the United States are truly, in their final extremity, fatherless and motherless. Abandoned to the abortionist's scalpel and vacuum, they have indeed become prey for the abortion industry, which grows ever richer with the blood money it receives from each unborn child it liquidates through abortion.

God creates each human soul and infuses it, at the moment of conception, in the unborn baby's body. To intentionally destroy that unborn life through abortion is murder—a grave sin—no matter what it may be called in polite society. And to be complicit in the perpetuation of the legalized murder of unborn babies through abortion is to be complicit in that sin.

Further Reading: Hosea 4:1–4; Isaiah 33:1; 45:10–12; Romans 1:28–32
CCC, 312, 1756, 2268–2272, 2322, 2260–2277, 2320–2321

21

Qualities of a Good Bishop

Saint Augustine, the magnificent fourth-century Church Father, has long been regarded as a model for bishops to emulate. A tireless shepherd and defender of his flock, Augustine embodied the essence of a great bishop.

A man of deep prayer and holiness, he was ascetical, Christ-centered, disciplined in his personal habits, joyful, wise, actively involved with the physical and spiritual welfare of his people and a dedicated and effective teacher. He understood that a primary duty of a bishop is to teach the faith, and teach he did, with amazing vigor and clarity. He wrote hundreds of substantive and brilliant works, all aimed at instructing and encouraging his fellow Catholics.

As a bishop, Saint Augustine was not afraid to teach. In that tumultuous and polarized era, when the formidable heresies of Donatism and Arianism wracked the Church, he indefatigably preached, wrote, admonished, defended, rebuked and consoled. He even engaged in public debates before large crowds with proponents of heresy, all in an effort to fulfill his duty as a shepherd of souls who defends his flock.

Here are some key scriptural passages that guided Saint Augustine in his efforts to be a good and holy bishop:

Titus 1:7–9 "For a bishop, as God's steward, must be blameless; he must not be arrogant or quick-tempered or a drunkard or violent or greedy for gain, but hospitable, a lover of goodness, master of himself, upright, holy, and self-controlled; he must hold firm to the sure word as taught, so that he may be able to give instruction in sound doctrine and also to confute those who contradict it."

1 Timothy 3:1–7 "If any one aspires to the office of bishop, he desires a noble task. Now a bishop must be above reproach, the husband of one wife, temperate, sensible, dignified, hospitable, an apt teacher, no drunkard, not violent but gentle, not quarrelsome, and no lover of money. He must manage his own household well, keeping his children submissive and respectful in every way; for if a man does not know how to manage his own household, how can he care for God's church? He must not be a recent convert, or he may be puffed up with conceit and fall into the condemnation of the devil; moreover he must be well thought of by outsiders, or he may fall into reproach and the snare of the devil."[1]

2 Timothy 4:1–5 "I charge you in the presence of God and of Christ Jesus who is to judge the living and the dead, and by his appearing and his kingdom: preach the word, be urgent in season and out of season, convince, rebuke, and exhort, be unfailing in patience and in teaching. For the time is coming when people will not endure sound teaching, but having itching ears they will accumulate for themselves teachers to suit their own likings, and will turn away from listening to the truth and wander into myths. As for you, always be steady, endure suffering, do the work of an evangelist, fulfil your ministry."

Augustine was also keenly aware of the Bible's warnings about unworthy shepherds, who through laziness or some other iniquity fail to live up to their duty. Here is a sobering example:

Jeremiah 23:1–4 "'Woe to the shepherds who destroy and scatter the sheep of my pasture!' says the Lord. Therefore thus says the LORD, the God of Israel, concerning the shepherds who care for my people: 'You have scattered my flock, and have driven them away, and you have not attended to them. Behold, I will attend to you for your evil doings,' says the LORD. 'Then I will gather the remnant of my flock out of all the countries where I have driven them, and I will bring them back to their fold, and they shall be fruitful and multiply. I will set shepherds over them who will care for them, and they shall fear no more, nor be dismayed, neither shall any be missing,' says the LORD."

(For a particularly ominous warning to bad shepherds [and bishops], read Ezekiel 34:1–16!)

Knowing he would one day give an account to God for his time as bishop, Saint Augustine wrote, "While I am frightened by what I am to you, I am also consoled by what I share with you. *To* you I am a bishop, *with* you I am a Christian. The first is an office, the second is a grace; the first a danger, the second salvation." [2]

Let's pray fervently, every day, for our bishops, asking God to bless and strengthen them, giving them the graces they need to be courageous and effective shepherds. After all, they carry a very heavy load on their shoulders—us!

Further Reading: Jeremiah 50:3–6; Ezekiel 34:1–16;
1 Timothy 3:1–7; 5:22; Hebrews 5:1–4; 1 Peter 5:1–5
CCC, 873–896, 1555–1561

22

What's Up With the Rapture?

Thanks to the proliferation of the wildly popular (and wildly problematic) *Left Behind* books, many Christians, including some Catholics, believe in the "rapture." The rapture theory holds that Christ will come silently, in a hidden way, to remove born-again believers from this world just before the Great Tribulation, when the Antichrist (Matthew 24:11) and the Beast (Revelation 13, 17) rise to cause global havoc and bloodshed.

The rapture theory as we know it today first appeared toward the end of the nineteenth century among some American Protestants who were fixated on the end times. Prior to the nineteenth century, the popular notion of a rapture was simply unheard of among Christians.

Let's consider the five major Bible verses cited as proof-texts by those who believe in a pre-tribulation rapture.

1 Thessalonians 4:16–17 "For the Lord Himself will descend from heaven with a cry of command, with the archangel's call, and with the sound of the trumpet of God. And the dead in Christ will rise first; then we who are alive, who are left, shall be caught up together with them in the clouds to meet the Lord in the air; and so we shall always be with the Lord."

First, notice that this passage refers to the Second Coming of Christ and says nothing about a secret or hidden coming of Christ. Second, this event is public and audible—exactly the opposite of a hidden coming of Christ that those who promote the rapture theory assert. They claim that Christ will appear secretly and will be seen only by those who are raptured. But such a notion completely clashes with 1 Thessalonians 4. It is another example of reading into the biblical text something that simply isn't there.

Matthew 24:37–42 "As were the days of Noah, so will be the coming of the Son of man. For as in those days before the flood they were eating and drinking, marrying and giving in marriage, until the day when Noah entered the ark, and they did not know until the flood came and swept them all away, so will be the coming of the Son of man. Then two men will be in the field; one is taken and one is left. Two women will be grinding at the mill; one is taken and one is left. Watch therefore, for you do not know on what day your Lord is coming."

Christ seems to be referring to the destruction of Jerusalem in AD 70. Earlier in Matthew 24, he warned that "*this* generation will not pass away till all these things take place" (v. 34, emphasis added). He also said that this event would be "just like the days of Noah." But notice that the people "taken away" in Noah's day were the unrighteous, not the righteous (Genesis 6 and 7). The righteous—Noah and his family—were "left behind." This is the exact opposite of the rapture theory.

And don't forget that Christ promised that the one "who *endures to the end* will be saved" (Matthew 24:13, emphasis added). This includes those Christians who will endure the Tribulation.

1 Corinthians 15:51–52 "Lo! I tell you a mystery. We shall not all sleep, but we shall all be changed, in a moment, in the twinkling of an eye, at the last trumpet. For the trumpet will sound, and the dead will be raised imperishable, and we shall be changed."

Again, this passage refers to the Second Coming of Christ. The "twinkling of an eye" refers to the instantaneous change from a mortal body to a glorified body (1 Corinthians 15:23), not to the speed of the rapture. In fact, this verse can't refer to the rapture because it specifically connects this event to the blast of the "last trumpet," which heralds Christ's Second Coming (Matthew 24:30–31). The Catholic Church has consistently interpreted this passage as such for the last two thousand years.

Revelation 3:10 "Because you [i.e., the Church at Philadelphia] have kept my word of patient endurance, I will keep you from the hour of trial that is coming on the whole world to test the inhabitants of the earth" (NRSV).

Once again, we see a passage that refers to the Second Coming of Christ, not a secret coming beforehand. But does the phrase "keep you from the hour of testing" mean that the Church will be "removed" before the Tribulation begins? No. There are many Bible verses that show that Christ permits his Church to suffer persecution and tribulation. In John 17:15 Christ says, "I do *not* pray that thou shouldst take them out of the world, but that thou shouldst keep them from the evil one" (emphasis added). John 16:33 says, "In the world you have tribulation; but be of good cheer, I have overcome the world." John 15:19 says that Christians have been *chosen* "out of the world," but it does not say that Christians will be *taken* out of the world prior to a time of persecution (see Matthew 10:16–33).

The Church will endure persecutions and tribulations (Matthew 24:21; CCC, 675) and it will come through them purified (Romans 12:12; 2 Corinthians 4:4; 1 Thessalonians 3:4; Revelation 1:9; 2:10; 7:14).

Revelation 4:1–2 "After this I looked, and lo, in heaven an open door! And the first voice, which I had heard speaking to me like a trumpet, said, 'Come up hither, and I will show you what must take place after this.' At once I was in the Spirit, and lo, a throne stood in heaven, with one seated on the throne!" Many rapture believers argue that in this passage John symbolizes the Church (though they deny that he could symbolize the Church when Christ told him, "Son, behold your mother" [John 19:26–27]). They claim that John, when he is commanded to "come up here" represents the Church being raptured into heaven.

But there's a big problem here. In the book of Revelation, Saint John comes back to earth *after* he is told to "come up here" to heaven. In Revelation 17 he returns to earth and sees the Whore of Babylon astride the seven-headed, ten-horned Beast. The Whore of Babylon could not be in heaven; she is on earth. Then Saint John is sent to "a great and high mountain," where he watches the heavenly Jerusalem coming down to earth, "out of heaven" (Revelation 21:10).

The Catholic Church rejects the rapture theory for good reasons. It is unbiblical and completely alien to the historic Christian tradition surrounding the Second Coming of Christ. Remember that Christ said he would return on "the last day" (John 6:39–40) to judge the living and the dead (see also Matthew 24 and 25). There will be no secret or hidden coming in the meantime. When the Lord returns, you'll definitely know about it.

Further Reading: Joel 2:31; Ezekiel 13:5; Isaiah 2:12; Matthew 5:22; 7:1–5; 11:20–24; 12:41–42; 24:12; Mark 12:38–40; Luke 12:1–3; 18:8; John 3:20–21; Acts 10:42; Romans 2:5–16; 14:10; 1 Corinthians 4:5; 15:23; 2 Corinthians 5:10; 1 Thessalonians 5:2–3; 2 Thessalonians 2:4–12; 2 Timothy 4:1; 1 Peter 4:5;

2 Peter 3:12–13; 1 John 2:18–22; 2 John 7; Revelation 13:8;
19:1–9; 20:7–10; 21:2–4
CCC, 524, 668–682, 830, 865, 1001, 1186, 1200

23

Follow Your Conscience

We've all heard the catchphrase, "You have to follow your conscience." Unfortunately, many people are under the mistaken impression that "following my conscience" means "doing what I want to do."

Consider, for example, a married woman who asks her Catholic friend for advice on whether it's permissible for her and her husband to use contraception. The friend might tell her, "You have to follow your conscience." But if she offers no further explanation of what conscience is and how it works, the woman will likely assume from this advice that what she *wants* to do in this regard is the voice of her conscience. And that, of course, would be a mistake.

While it's absolutely true that each of us must *always* follow our conscience (CCC, 1790), we must also recognize that each of us has the obligation to properly form (that is, educate) our conscience (CCC, 1783–1785).

The *Catechism* explains:

"Deep within his conscience man discovers a law which he has not laid upon himself but which he must obey. Its voice, ever calling him to love and to do what is good and to avoid evil, sounds in his heart at the right moment.... For man has in his heart a law inscribed by

God.... His conscience is man's most secret core and his sanctuary. There he is alone with God whose voice echoes in his depths" [GS 16]. (CCC, 1776)

Our conscience, it therefore follows, is what enables us

to do good and to avoid evil. It also judges particular choices, approving those that are good and denouncing those that are evil [cf. *Rom* 1:32]. It bears witness to the authority of truth in reference to the supreme Good to which the human person is drawn, and it welcomes the commandments. When he listens to his conscience, the prudent man can hear God speaking.

Conscience is a judgment of reason whereby the human person recognizes the moral quality of a concrete act that he is going to perform, is in the process of performing, or has already completed. In all he says and does, man is obliged to follow faithfully what he knows to be just and right. It is by the judgment of his conscience that man perceives and recognizes the prescriptions of the divine law.... (CCC, 1777–1778)

With these teachings in mind, let's examine some of what Scripture says about the joy of a clear conscience contrasted with the misery of a guilty conscience.

We'll begin with Adam and Eve and their original sin. As you can see from Adam's response to God, their guilty consciences were bothering them. (Sound familiar?)

Genesis 3:7–10 "Then the eyes of both were opened, and they knew that they were naked; and they sewed fig leaves together and made themselves aprons. And they heard the sound of the LORD God walking in the garden in the cool of the day, and the man and his wife hid themselves from the presence of the LORD God among the trees of the garden. But the LORD God called to the man, and said to him, 'Where are you?' And he said, 'I heard the sound of thee in the garden, and I was afraid, because I was naked; and I hid myself.'"

Wisdom of Solomon 17:11–13 "For wickedness is a cowardly thing, condemned by its own testimony; / distressed by conscience, it has always exaggerated the difficulties. / For fear is nothing but surrender of the helps that come from reason; / and the inner expectation of help, being weak, / prefers ignorance of what causes the torment."

Isaiah 48:22 "'There is no peace,' says the LORD, 'for the wicked.'" This warning gets right to the heart of the matter, and serves two purposes. First, it shows us that good living will lead to a clear conscience and lack of stress over past sins. And second, it points us to the fact that in eternity those who have loved God and tried to live according to his teachings will enjoy peace. Conversely, those who spurn God's laws and live wickedly will suffer for eternity with no peace of soul. And *that* will be hell.

Proverbs 10:8–9 "The wise of heart will heed commandments, but a prating fool will come to ruin. He who walks in integrity walks securely, / but he who perverts his ways will be found out."

1 Timothy 1:18–19 "This charge I commit to you, Timothy, my son,…[that] you may wage the good warfare, holding faith and a good conscience. By rejecting conscience, certain persons have made shipwreck of their faith."

Romans 2:13–16 "[I]t is not the hearers of the law who are righteous before God, but the doers of the law who will be justified. When Gentiles who have not the law do by nature what the law requires, they are a law to themselves, even though they do not have the law. They show that what the law requires is written on their hearts, while their conscience also bears witness and their conflicting thoughts accuse or perhaps excuse them on that day when, according to my gospel, God judges the secrets of men by Christ Jesus."

1 John 3:19–22 "By this we shall know that we are of the truth, and reassure our hearts before him whenever our hearts condemn us; for God is greater than our hearts, and he knows everything. Beloved, if our hearts do not condemn us, we have confidence before God; and we receive from him whatever we ask, because we keep his commandments and do what pleases him."

Further Reading: Deuteronomy 28:65–67; Job 15:20–25; 27:6; Proverbs 3:21–25; 15:14–15, 28:1; Psalm 112:5–10; Sirach 34:13–16; Luke 23:30; John 3:20–21; Romans 2:9; 1 Timothy 1:5; 3:8–9; Hebrews 10:22; 1 Peter 3:15–16 CCC, 1776–1802

24

Gluttony

Remember that 1970s TV commercial for Alka-Seltzer? A visibly nauseous man groans, "I can't believe I ate the whole thing." His wife chides him saying, "You ate it."

That commercial can be a useful, if humorous, reminder of the dangers of overeating. Christians know eating or drinking to excess as *gluttony*. In addition to causing undesirable physical side effects, such as obesity, diseases and a dulling of the will and intellect, gluttony also causes negative spiritual side effects. This is why Pope Saint Gregory the Great called gluttony a "capital" sin, because it causes a variety of other sins to spring up in its wake.

Keep in mind that although we rightly associate gluttony specifically with immoderation in food and drink, it is a spiritual disorder that can apply to created things in general, not just food. When one excessively indulges the sensual appetite for any thing—food, wine, sex, entertainment—one becomes gluttonous. And while it is commonly understood that gluttony is not typically a mortal sin (though it is always at least a venial sin), it is especially dangerous because it is often the cause of other, worse sins.

Saint Thomas Aquinas taught that "Gluttony denotes, not any desire of eating and drinking, but an inordinate desire." It arises from an "immoderate pleasure in eating and drinking."[1] This means that eating in itself is not the problem. We all have to eat to stay alive. Rather, it's when we willfully give in to an inordinate or immoderate (i.e., excessive) appetite for food that we start entering the territory of sin.

Speaking about people whose focus is only on sensual, earthly pleasures, Saint Paul warned, "Brethren, join in imitating me, and mark those who so live as you have an example in us. For many, of whom I have often told you and now tell you even with tears, live as enemies of the cross of Christ. Their end is destruction, *their god is the belly*, and they glory in their shame, with minds set on earthly things" (Philippians 3:17–19, emphasis added).

Saint Paul's phrase, "their god is the belly," is a vivid description of the fundamental problem with gluttony: It tends to make a created thing—in this case, food—into a god. And when this tendency becomes so entrenched, and when a person becomes so focused on the pleasure of eating food that it has become, in a sense, an object of lust for the appetite, then in truth one can become a slave to his or her senses.

Gluttony, one of the seven capital vices, has as its opposite temperance, which is one of the four cardinal virtues. The key is to realize that if you have a problem with gluttony, you can, with God's grace, overcome it by cultivating the virtue of temperance, or moderation, in your eating and drinking. One Catholic writer explained moderation as "the righteous habit which makes a man govern his natural appetite for pleasures of the senses in accordance with the norm prescribed by reason."[2]

Scripture contains numerous warnings about the dangers of gluttony and immoderation as well as the beauty of temperance and self-control:

Sirach 37:27–31 "My son, test your soul while you live; / see what is bad for it and do not give it that. / For not everything is good for every one, / and not every person enjoys everything. / Do not have an insatiable appetite for any luxury, / and do not give yourself up to food; / for overeating brings sickness, / and gluttony leads to nausea. / Many have died of gluttony, / but he who is careful to avoid it prolongs his life."

Luke 21:34–35 "But take heed to yourselves lest your hearts be weighed down with dissipation and drunkenness and cares of this life, and that day come upon you suddenly like a snare; for it will come upon all who dwell upon the face of the whole earth." The Greek word used here for "dissipation" is *kraipále*, which can be translated more literally as "surfeiting," a fancy word for "overdoing it" with food and drink. Christ teaches us here that people who are focused on sensuality will be unprepared for that sudden and unexpected moment when they die and stand before Christ the Judge to render to him an account of their lives (Matthew 25:31–46; Luke 12:16–20; Romans 14:12).

1 Corinthians 6:12–13, 19–20 "'All things are lawful for me,' but not all things are helpful. 'All things are lawful for me,' but I will not be enslaved by anything. 'Food is meant for the stomach and the stomach for food'—and God will destroy both one and the other. The body is not meant for immorality, but for the Lord, and the Lord for the body.... Do you not know that your body is a temple of the Holy Spirit within you, which you have from God? You are not your own; you were bought with a price. So glorify God in your body."

Romans 13:11–14 "Besides this you know what hour it is, how it is full time now for you to wake from sleep. For salvation is nearer to us now than when we first believed; the night is far gone, the day is at hand. Let us then cast off the works of darkness and put on the armor of light; let us conduct ourselves becomingly as in the day, not in reveling and drunkenness, not in debauchery and licentiousness, not in quarreling and jealousy. But put on the Lord

Jesus Christ, and *make no provision for the flesh, to gratify its desires"* (emphasis added).

Further Reading: Deuteronomy 21:20; Proverbs 21:17; 23:19–21; 28:7; Matthew 11:19; Luke 7:34; Romans 12:1–2; Galatians 5:19–21; Titus 1:12
CCC, 1866, 2290, 2535

25

Do Catholics "Keep Christ on the Cross"?

Many non-Catholics have an aversion to crucifixes. While they have no problem with an "empty cross," some (Protestants, for example) object to the crucifix because it depicts Christ dying on the cross. "Christ isn't on the cross anymore," they say. "He's reigning gloriously in heaven. So why emphasize his death?" This is a reasonable question, and it deserves a reasonable answer.

Let's start by recognizing that Catholics emphasize both the Crucifixion and the Resurrection, not minimizing or downplaying the importance of either. In our manger scenes, stained glass windows and statues, we also depict the Lord as a baby in the manger, as a toddler in his mother's arms and as a young man teaching the rabbis in the temple. Each of these stages of the Lord's life is worthy of depiction. But the *focal point and purpose* of Christ's Incarnation and ministry is his death on the cross. As he himself said, "For this I was born, and for this I have come into the world, to bear witness to the truth" (John 18:37).

On his popular TV show, *Life Is Worth Living*, Archbishop Fulton Sheen summarized the reason for using a crucifix instead of an empty cross: "Keep your eyes on the crucifix, for Jesus without the cross is a man without a mission, and the cross without Jesus is a burden without a reliever."

Isn't it true that when you see an empty cross, your mind automatically "sees" Christ there? After all, we recognize that the cross only has meaning because Christ died on it for our salvation. Catholics use crucifixes to avoid what Saint Paul warned about—the cross being "emptied of its power" (1 Corinthians 1:17).

Christ's supreme act was to die on the cross as atonement for our sins. His Resurrection was proof that what he did on the cross worked—he conquered death—and it demonstrated beyond any doubt that he was who he claimed to be: God. The Crucifixion was the act that changed history. The Resurrection demonstrated the efficacy of that act.

By his death on the cross, Christ conquered sin and death, redeemed the world, opened the way of salvation for all who would receive it and reconciled his people with the Father (Ephesians 2:13–18; Colossians 1:19–20). That is why the crucifix is such a potent reminder for us of what he did on our behalf that dark afternoon on Calvary.

"Jesus told his disciples, 'If any man would come after me, let him deny himself and take up his cross and follow me'" (Matthew 16:24; see Matthew 10:38). True, resurrection and glory await all those who follow Christ faithfully—but we will only arrive there by traveling the way of the cross.

Saint Paul emphasized the Crucifixion, saying, "When I came to you, brethren, I did not come proclaiming to you the testimony of God in lofty words or wisdom. *For I decided to know nothing among you except Jesus Christ and him crucified*" (1 Corinthians 2:1–2, emphasis added).

And in 1 Corinthians 1:18–24 Saint Paul said, "For the word of the cross is folly to those who are perishing, but to us who are being saved it is the power of God.... [I]t pleased God through the folly of what we preach to save those who believe. For Jews demand signs and Greeks seek wisdom, *but we preach Christ crucified*, a stumbling block to Jews and folly to Gentiles, but to those who are called, both Jews and Greeks, Christ the power of God and the wisdom of God" (emphasis added).

In Galatians 6:14 he proclaimed: "But far be it from me to glory except in the cross of our Lord Jesus Christ, by which the world has been crucified to me, and I to the world."

And lest anyone imagine that the early Christians did not focus their minds on Christ's death on the cross, consider what Saint Paul says in 1 Corinthians 11:26, where he again emphasizes the Crucifixion: "For as often as you eat this bread and drink this cup, you proclaim the Lord's death until he comes."

Recall the scene of the Crucifixion: Some in the crowd present at Calvary shouted at Christ as he was dying, *"Come down off your cross!"* (see Matthew 27:40; Mark 15:30). What a strange and sad echo those words find today in objections to the crucifix as a reminder of Christ's sacrifice.

We Catholics should strive to emulate Saint Paul's resolution to "know nothing among you except Jesus Christ and him crucified" (1 Corinthians 2:2; see 1 Corinthians 1:17–18).

One way to deepen your appreciation of what Christ did for you on the cross is to stand or kneel before a crucifix while prayerfully reading the Gospel accounts of the Passion. Ponder also these poignant words:

> Victim of love, in manhood's prime
> Thou wilt ascend the Cross to die:
> Why hangs the Child before His time
> Stretched on that bed of agony?
> 'No thorn-wreath crowns My boyish brow
> No scourge has dealt its cruel smart

In hands and feet no nail-prints show
 No spear is planted in My heart.
'They have not set Me for a sign,
 Hung bare beneath the sunless sky,
Nor mixed the draught of gall and wine
 To mock My dying agony.
'The livelong night, the livelong day,
 My child, I travail for thy good,
And for thy sake I hang alway
 Self-crucified upon the Rood.
'To witness to the living Truth,
 To keep thee pure from sin's alloy,
I cloud the sunshine of My youth;
 The Man must suffer in the Boy.
'Visions of unrepented sin,
 The forfeit crown, the eternal loss,
Lie deep my sorrowing soul within,
 And nail My Body to the Cross.
'The livelong night, the livelong day,
 A Child upon that Cross I rest;
All night I for My children pray,
 All day I woo them to My breast.
'Long years of toil and pain are Mine,
 Ere I be lifted up to die,
Where cold the Paschal moonbeams shine
 At noon on darkened Calvary.
'Then will the thorn-wreath pierce My brow,
 The nails will fix Me to the tree;
But I shall hang as I do now,
 Self-crucified for love of thee!'[1]

(Henry Nutcombe Oxenham, "The Child-Christ on the Cross"
[1819–1888])

Further Reading: Matthew 10:37–39; 27:37; Luke 23:38;
John 3:1–4, 9 (compare with Numbers 21:8–9); 19:19;
Romans 6:1–10; 1 Corinthians 1:10–13; Galatians 2:20; 3:1;
5:24, 6:14.
CCC, 421, 469, 550, 555, 618, 766, 921, 1182, 1375, 2427, 2543

26

Purgatory

If Jesus Christ died 'once for all,'" a Protestant might query you, "then why does the Catholic Church teach that you must suffer in purgatory for your sins? Wasn't his death sufficient to save you from your sins?"

This is surely a reasonable question. After all, Hebrews 10:12–14 proclaims, "But when Christ had offered for all time a single sacrifice for sins, he sat down at the right hand of God, then to wait until his enemies should be made a stool for his feet. For by a single offering he has perfected for all time those who are sanctified." So, that being the case, how can purgatory be compatible with Christ's perfect, once-for-all sacrifice?

The key is to recognize that our earthly life affords us an opportunity to "be perfect, as your heavenly Father is perfect" (Matthew 5:48). We are called by Christ to accomplish this by his grace (Mark 9:23). He told us, "Blessed are the pure in heart, for they shall see God" (Matthew 5:8). These truths dovetail with what Revelation 21:27 says about the condition one must be in to enter heaven: "[N]othing unclean shall enter it."

Now, consider the words of Christ in Matthew 22:1–14. He compares heaven with a wedding feast. One of the invited guests arrives without a "wedding garment" (he is dressed shabbily and inappropriately for the great occasion). The master says to him,

"'Friend, how did you get in here without a wedding garment?' And he was speechless. Then the king said to the attendants, 'Bind him hand and foot, and cast him into the outer darkness; there men will weep and gnash their teeth.' For many are called, but few are chosen" (emphasis added).

Christ's once-for-all death on the cross is the perfect and unique sacrifice for sins, one that saves from damnation those who are in Christ (Hebrews 7:25) and "cleanses us from all sin" (1 John 1:7). But notice that this "cleansing" does not happen all at once; it takes time and perseverance on our part, for the span of our entire lives. Jesus said, "He who endures to the end will be saved" (Matthew 10:22; 24:13; Mark 13:13).

This all means that, for some of us, the process of purification in this life is left uncompleted when death comes. Hebrews 9:27 says, "[I]t is appointed for men to die once, and after that comes judgment." After the judgment comes our eternal destiny in either heaven or hell. For those whose names are found written in the Book of Life, heaven awaits. But since "nothing unclean" can enter the glorious splendor of God's presence in heaven (1 Timothy 6:16), if one is not fully prepared to meet God face-to-face, if spiritual defects and temporal effects of forgiven sins still cling to the soul, then some final purification must take place before that one can enter heaven.

Because God is all holy, the prophet Habakkuk reminds us, he will not allow anything in heaven with him to be less than holy and spotless: "Your eyes are too pure to behold evil [O Lord], / and you cannot look on wrongdoing" (1:13, NRSV). Catholics call this process of final purification or purgation "purgatory."

Saint Paul teaches very clearly in 1 Corinthians 3 that God performs a final purgation or purification—a process that involves suffering—on the souls of some departed Christians. This is the most central of all the biblical texts on purgatory and we will return to it later in this chapter. For the moment, though, read and ponder what the Bible says here about what happens to some souls when they are purified after death:

> According to the commission of God given to me, like a skilled master builder I laid a foundation, and someone else is building upon it. Let each one take care how he builds upon it. For no one can lay a foundation other than that which is laid, which is Jesus Christ. Now if anyone builds on the foundation with gold, silver, precious stones, wood, hay, straw—each one's work will become manifest; for the Day will disclose it, because it will be revealed by fire, and the fire will test what sort of work each one has done. If the work that anyone has built on the foundation survives, he will receive a reward. If anyone's work is burned up, he will suffer loss, though he himself will be saved, but only as through fire. (1 Corinthians 3:10–15, ESV)

This final purification removes all the dross that clings to the soul, things that Saint Paul describes metaphorically as "wood, hay, and straw"—flammable materials which are burned away in this judgment by God. Conversely, that man's good works—which Saint Paul compares with "gold, silver, and precious stones"—are refined and retained.

In Matthew 12:32, Christ mentions a sin that cannot be forgiven even "in the world to come," implying some sins will be forgiven after death.[1]

Remember Christ's parable about the unforgiving servant in Matthew 18:32–34? When the wicked servant proceeded to maltreat his fellow servant after the king had canceled his own debt, the king threw him into prison. "'You wicked servant! I forgave you all that debt because you besought me; and should not you have had mercy on your fellow servant, as I had mercy on you?' And in anger his lord delivered him to the jailers, till he should pay all his debt." Then Christ adds a chilling warning, meant for us: *"So also my heavenly Father will do to every one of you, if you do not forgive your brother from your heart"* (Matthew 18:35, emphasis added). Clearly, Christ did not mean that the Father would literally lock people in prison in this life; rather, he is referring to what will happen to those who die with a hard heart and stored-up anger, unwilling to forgive their brother or sister.

Those who die with these kinds of defects (and others of different types) adhering to the soul can and must be purified from them. Only then will they be able to enter into glory, the presence of God himself.

Further Reading: 2 Maccabees 12:43-45; Luke 16:19–31; 1 Corinthians 11:27–32; Hebrews 11:13–16, 32–40; 1 Peter 3:18–19; 4:6
CCC, 1030–1032, 1472–1477

27

Do Good Works Work?

The question of whether or not Christ requires good works for salvation is a vexing and long-standing matter of dispute between many Catholics and Protestants. While it would be utterly impossible to explain this issue adequately within this limited space, it is helpful for Catholics and Protestants to consider those Scripture passages that tell us something about the role good works play in Christ's plan of salvation.

Matthew 7:21–26 "Not every one who says to me, 'Lord, Lord,' shall enter the kingdom of heaven, but *he who does the will of my Father who is in heaven*.... Every one then who hears these words of mine *and does them* will be like a wise man who built his house upon the rock.... And every one who hears these words of mine *and does not do them* will be like a foolish man who built his house upon the sand" (emphasis added).

Matthew 19:16–22 "And behold, one came up to him, saying, 'Teacher, what good deed must I do, to have eternal life?' And he said to him, 'Why do you ask me about what is good? One there is who is good. *If you would enter life, keep the commandments*'" (emphasis added).

Matthew 25:31–41 "When the Son of man comes in his glory, and all the angels with him, then he will sit on his glorious throne.

Before him will be gathered all the nations, and he will separate them one from another as a shepherd separates the sheep from the goats, and he will place the sheep at his right hand, but the goats at the left. Then the King will say to those at his right hand, 'Come, O blessed of my Father, inherit the kingdom prepared for you from the foundation of the world; for I was hungry and you gave me food, I was thirsty and you gave me drink, I was a stranger and you welcomed me, I was naked and you clothed me, I was sick and you visited me, I was in prison and you came to me.'"

Romans 2:2–10 "We know that the judgment of God rightly falls upon those who do such things.... *For he will render to every man according to his works*: to those who by patience in well-doing [i.e., in doing good works] seek for glory and honor and immortality, he will give eternal life; but for those who are factious and *do not obey the truth*, but obey wickedness, there will be wrath and fury. There will be tribulation and distress for every human being who does evil…but glory and honor and peace for every one who does good" (emphasis added).

Galatians 5:6 "For in Christ Jesus neither circumcision nor uncircumcision is of any avail, but *faith working through love*" (emphasis added).

Philippians 2:12–13 "Therefore, my beloved, as you have always obeyed, so now, not only as in my presence but much more in my absence, *work out your own salvation with fear and trembling*; for God is at work in you, both to will and to work for his good pleasure" (emphasis added).

Ephesians 2:8–10 "For by grace you have been saved through faith; and this is not your own doing, it is the gift of God—not because of works, lest any man should boast. For we are his workmanship, created in Christ Jesus for good works, which God prepared beforehand, that we should walk in them."

James 2:14–17 "What does it profit, my brethren, if a man says he has faith but has not works? Can his faith save him? If a brother or sister is ill-clad and in lack of daily food, and one of you says to them, 'Go in peace, be warmed and filled,' without giving them the things needed for the body, what does it profit? *So faith by itself, if it has no works, is dead*" (emphasis added).

James 2:20–24 "*Do you want to be shown, you foolish fellow, that faith apart from works is barren?* Was not Abraham our father justified by works, when he offered his son Isaac upon the altar? You see that faith was active along with his works, and faith was completed by works, and the scripture was fulfilled which says, 'Abraham believed God, and it was reckoned to him as righteousness'; and he was called the friend of God. You see *that a man is justified by works and not by faith alone*" (emphasis added).

Revelation 2:26 "He who conquers *and who keeps my works until the end*, I will give him power over the nations" (emphasis added).

1 John 3:21 "Beloved, if our hearts do not condemn us, we have confidence before God; and we receive from him whatever we ask, *because we keep his commandments and do what pleases him*. And this is his commandment, *that we should believe in the name of his Son Jesus Christ and love one another, just as he has commanded us*. All who keep his commandments abide in him, and he in them" (emphasis added).

1 John 5:2 "By this we know that *we love the children of God, when we love God and obey his commandments*. For this is the love of God, that we keep his commandments" (emphasis added).

Further Reading: Matthew 5:16; Luke 1:5–6; John 6:28; 9:4; 14:22; Acts 9:36; Romans 3:20–28; Hebrews 10:24; Revelation 2:2–5; 2:19–23

28

Guardian Angels

Do you ever think about your guardian angel? You have one, you know. Your angel's mission from God is to look after you. This role is explained in the simple prayer that Catholics everywhere learn in childhood:

Angel of God my guardian dear,
to whom God's love commits me here,
Ever this day be at my side,
to light and guard, to rule and guide.

Amen.

Interestingly, the ancient and much-cherished Catholic belief in guardian angels—mighty spirits charged by God to assist human beings—has never been formally defined as a dogma of the Church. It has, however, always been part of Catholic belief and piety. The Catholic Church's two thousand-year history of liturgy, prayers, hymns and sacred art has been filled with the presence of belief in guardian angels—and for good reason. The Old Testament contains numerous examples of God assigning angels to protect and deliver his people. And, as you might expect, we see similar incidents of angelic protection in the New Testament as well.

The Lord himself explicitly taught the existence of guardian angels when he said, "See that you do not despise one of these little ones; for I tell you that in heaven their angels always behold the face of my Father who is in heaven" (Matthew 18:10).

Genesis 19 recounts the case of two angels sent by God to protect Lot and his family from a violent mob bent on harming or killing them. These angels not only struck many of the aggressors with blindness, but they also spirited Lot and his family out of the city just before God rained down a hail of flaming brimstone upon it, obliterating it and its wicked inhabitants for the terrible iniquities committed there (see Luke 17:29).

In Exodus 32:34 God promised Moses and the Israelites a special guardian angel saying, "my angel shall go before you."

In Daniel 10 a warrior angel is sent to speak with the prophet Daniel. This angel had a "face like the appearance of lightning, his eyes like flaming torches, his arms and legs like the gleam of burnished bronze, and the sound of his words like the noise of a multitude" (v. 6). The angel explained to Daniel that he was fighting alongside "Michael" (that is, Saint Michael the Archangel) against the "Prince of Persia" (a wicked angel that oppressed the people of that region) (Daniel 10:13).

The Deuterocanonical book of Tobit contains yet another account of a guardian angel, Raphael, who was sent by God to guide and protect the virtuous Hebrew youths Tobiah and Sarah (Tobit 3:16–17; see also chapters 5—6; 8—9; 12). At one point, the angel Raphael defeats the wicked angel Asmodeus, a demon, and "binds him hand and foot" (Tobit 8:3).

Here are several other scriptural reminders that God does indeed send his holy angels to light and guard, to rule and guide his people.

Psalm 91:9–12 "Because you have made the LORD your refuge, / the Most High your habitation, / no evil shall befall you, / no scourge come near your tent. / For he will give his angels charge of you / to guard you in all your ways. / On their hands they will bear you up, / lest you dash your foot against a stone."

Exodus 23:20–22 "Behold, I send an angel before you, to guard you on the way and to bring you to the place which I have prepared. Give heed to him and hearken to his voice, do not rebel against him, for he will not pardon your transgression; for my name is in him. But if you hearken attentively to his voice and do all that I say, then I will be an enemy to your enemies and an adversary to your adversaries."

Psalm 34:7 "The angel of the LORD encamps around those who fear him, and delivers them."

Daniel 6:19–22 "[T]he king arose and went in haste to the den of lions. When he came near to the den where Daniel was, he cried out in a tone of anguish and said to Daniel, 'O Daniel, servant of the living God, has your God, whom you serve continually, been able to deliver you from the lions?' Then Daniel said to the king, 'O king, live for ever! My God sent his angel and shut the lions' mouths, and they have not hurt me, because I was found blameless before him; and also before you, O king, I have done no wrong.'"

Acts 12:13–16 "And when he [Peter] knocked at the door of the gateway, a maid named Rhoda came to answer. Recognizing Peter's voice, in her joy she did not open the gate but ran in and told that Peter was standing at the gate. They said to her, 'You are mad.' But she insisted that it was so. They said, '*It is his angel!*' But Peter continued knocking; and when they opened, they saw him and were amazed" (emphasis added). This passage indicates that the New Testament-era Christians believed in guardian angels.

Hebrews 1:14 "Are not all ministering spirits [angels] sent forth to serve, for the sake of those who are to obtain salvation?"

Further Reading: Genesis 24:7; Numbers 20:14–16; Psalm 34:8; 35:5; 2 Maccabees 3:22–28; 10:29–30; 11:6; 15:23–24; Zechariah 1:8–11; 3:6–7; Judith 13:20; Acts 5:18–23; 12:6–11
CCC, 328–336

29

Are You a *Bad* Samaritan?

We all know the story of the Good Samaritan (Luke 10:29–37). In this beloved parable Christ teaches us the importance and virtue of attending to the needs of others, especially when doing so involves sacrifice. The Lord's message is clear: We should each strive to emulate the Good Samaritan, exercising selfless charity by helping others whenever opportunities arise. But have you ever considered the other side of the coin: what it means to be a *bad* Samaritan?

A bad Samaritan is one who sees the needs of others and whether because of laziness, greed, prejudice, pride or some other failing, refuses to help. A bad Samaritan recognizes that he should help someone out of a predicament but does nothing. A bad Samaritan is one who, by his refusal to help others, commits sins of omission. In the *Confiteor* at Mass, we publicly proclaim:

"I confess to Almighty God, and to you, my brothers and sisters, that I have sinned through my own fault, in my thoughts and in my words, in what I have done *and what I have failed to do.*"

Perhaps the earliest biblical example of hard-heartedness toward others is found in Genesis 4:9, with Cain's smart-aleck retort to God's question: "Then the LORD said to Cain, 'Where is Abel your brother?' He said, 'I do not know; *am I my brother's keeper?*'" (emphasis added).

Matthew 25:41–46 "Christ promised that one day he would return to judge the world. On that day, the good and the wicked will be separated like sheep and goats. Those who are destined for heaven will be rewarded for clothing the naked, giving drink to the thirsty, and visiting the imprisoned. But to the wicked he will say, 'Depart from me, you cursed, into the eternal fire prepared for the devil and his angels; for I was hungry and you gave me no food, I was thirsty and you gave me no drink, I was a stranger and you did not welcome me, naked and you did not clothe me, sick and in prison and you did not visit me.' Then they also will answer, 'Lord, when did we see thee hungry or thirsty or a stranger or naked or sick or in prison, and did not minister to thee?' Then he will answer them, 'Truly, I say to you, as you did it not to one of the least of these, you did it not to me.' And they will go away into eternal punishment, but the righteous into eternal life."

Deuteronomy 15:7–9 "If there is among you a poor man, one of your brethren, in any of your towns within your land which the LORD your God gives you, you shall not harden your heart or shut your hand against your poor brother, but you shall open your hand to him, and lend him sufficient for his need, whatever it may be. Take heed lest there be a base [i.e., selfish] thought in your heart, and you say, 'The seventh year, the year of release is near,' and your eye be hostile to your poor brother, and you give him nothing, and he cry to the LORD against you, and it be sin in you."

Proverbs 14:31 "He who oppresses a poor man insults his Maker, / but he who is kind to the needy honors him."

James 2:14–17, 20 "What does it profit, my brethren, if a man says he has faith but has not works? Can his faith save him? If a brother or sister is ill-clad and in lack of daily food, and one of you says to them, 'Go in peace, be warmed and filled,' without giving them the things needed for the body, what does it profit? So faith by itself, if it has no works, is dead.... Do you want to be shown, you foolish fellow, that faith apart from works is barren?" (The Greek word used here for barren, *nekra*, literally means "dead.")

And finally, consider this warning in 1 John 3:14–17:

> We know that we have passed out of death into life, because we love the brethren. He who does not love remains in death. Any one who hates his brother is a murderer, and you know that no murderer has eternal life abiding in him. By this we know love, that he laid down his life for us; and we ought to lay down our lives for the brethren. But if any one has the world's goods and sees his brother in need, yet closes his heart against him, how does God's love abide in him?

Further Reading: Exodus 22:21–24; Leviticus 25:35; Job 34:19; Proverbs 14:21; 29:7; Amos 4:1; 8:5–6; Psalms 9:18; 68:10; 102:17; 146:7; Matthew 6:1; 7:21; 19:21; Luke 21:4; Acts 4:34–37; 2 Corinthians 9:7; Galatians 2:10; Hebrews 10:24; Revelation 3:16; James 5:4
CCC, 678, 1853, 1969–1970, 2094, 2445

30

"Hell? No? We Won't Go?"

No one wants to receive bad news. The worse the news, the worse one feels. A harrowing example of someone who got the absolute *worst* news possible is found amid the paintings that adorn the Vatican's Sistine Chapel. The scene depicts the soul of a sinner who has been judged and is being dragged downward by gleeful demons into the fires of hell. His look of horrified stupefaction, as he realizes that he will spend all eternity in hell, is beyond adequate description.

The haunting visage of that damned soul's despair should remind us of why we Catholics pray: *"Oh my Jesus, forgive us our sins and save us from the fires of hell. Lead all souls to heaven, especially those most in need of thy mercy."*

The *Catechism* reminds us that the Catholic Church "affirms the existence of hell and its eternity" (1035). Those who die in mortal sin are destined for hell, the "eternal fire" that Christ warned of in the Gospel of Matthew (25:41, 46). A major aspect of the suffering of hell is the excruciating desolation of knowing that you will be eternally separated from God, the one by whom and for whom each one of us was created and for whom we long for all eternity (CCC, 1035).

Sacred Scripture bristles with many grim reminders that hell is a real place where real people go. It awaits those who spurn God's grace and mercy, commit mortal sins and, tragically, die unrepentant in the state of mortal sin. Before we examine some of those biblical warnings about hell, let's take a moment to remember that no one goes to hell unless they *choose* to.

Hell is the *bad* news. But let's praise and thank our Lord that there's also very Good News, the gospel of Jesus Christ, which promises that the one who loves God (Matthew 22:37), believes and trusts in his grace and mercy (Acts 16:30–31), and strives to live according to his teachings (Matthew 7:21–23; John 14:15) will not go to hell. All those who die in the state of grace will be with God in heaven for all eternity. Which means, conversely, that all those who don't find themselves in that state when they die will go to hell. Let's look at what the Bible says about this.

Matthew 25 This chapter is entirely dedicated to Christ's teaching on the existence and pains of hell. The "foolish virgins" (vv. 1–13), the "wicked and slothful servant" (vv. 14–30) and the "goats" (vv. 31–33) whom Christ condemns for their failure to love their neighbor, each exemplify men and women who go to hell—a place of "eternal fire prepared for the devil and his angels" (v. 41), a place of "darkness" where they will "weep and gnash their teeth" (v. 30).

Isaiah 33:14 "The sinners in Zion are afraid; / trembling has seized the godless: / 'Who among us can dwell with the devouring fire? / Who among us can dwell with everlasting burnings?'"

Matthew 3:12 "[God's] winnowing fork is in his hand, and he will clear his threshing floor and gather his wheat into the granary, but the chaff he will burn with unquenchable fire."

Mark 9:43–48 "And if your hand causes you to sin, cut it off; it is better for you to enter life maimed than with two hands to go to hell, to the unquenchable fire. And if your foot causes you to sin, cut it off; it is better for you to enter life lame than with two feet to be thrown into hell. And if your eye causes you to sin, pluck it out; it is better for you to enter the kingdom of God with one eye than with two eyes to be thrown into hell, where their worm does not die, and the fire is not quenched."

Luke 12:5 "I tell you, my friends, do not fear those who kill the body, and after that have no more that they can do. But I will warn you whom to fear: fear him who, after he has killed, has power to cast into hell; yes, I tell you, fear him!"

2 Thessalonians 1:5–10 "This is evidence of the righteous judgment of God…when the Lord Jesus is revealed from heaven with his mighty angels in flaming fire, inflicting vengeance upon those who do not know God and upon those who do not obey the gospel of our Lord Jesus. They shall suffer the punishment of eternal destruction and exclusion from the presence of the Lord and from the glory of his might, when he comes on that day to be glorified in his saints."

Revelation 20:11–15 "Then I saw a great white throne and him who sat upon it; from his presence earth and sky fled away, and no place was found for them. And I saw the dead, great and small, standing before the throne, and books were opened. Also another book was opened, which is the book of life. And the dead were judged by what was written in the books, by what they had done. And the sea gave up the dead in it, Death and Hades gave up the dead in them, and all were judged by what they had done. Then Death and Hades were thrown into the lake of fire. This is the second death, the lake of fire; and if any one's name was not found written in the book of life, he was thrown into the lake of fire."

Revelation 21:5–8 "And he who sat upon the throne said…'I am the Alpha and the Omega, the beginning and the end. To the thirsty I will give water without price from the fountain of the water of life. He who conquers shall have this heritage, and I will be his God and he shall be my son. But as for the cowardly, the faithless, the polluted, as for murderers, fornicators, sorcerers, idolaters, and all liars, their lot shall be in the lake that burns with fire and brimstone, which is the second death."

Further Reading: Daniel 12:2; Job 10:20–22; 21; Judith 16:21; Psalm 21:8–9; Matthew 5:21–30; 10:28; 23:15; Luke 16:22–26; Romans 2:6–9; 1 Corinthians 6:9; Hebrews 10:26–31; James 3:6; 2 Peter 2:4; Jude 1:6, 13; Revelation 9:1–2; 14:9–11; 19:20 CCC, 1033–1041

31

Infant Baptism

In order to better understand why, since the days of the Apostles, the Catholic Church has always and everywhere baptized babies, we must first understand what baptism does.

Christ told us, "Truly, truly, I say to you, unless one is born of water and the Spirit, he cannot enter the kingdom of God" (John 3:5). The earliest Christians understood him to mean that being "born anew" by water and the Holy Spirit refers to the sacrament of baptism, and they lived out that understanding by baptizing themselves and their children, including their infants. They understood that the sacrament of baptism is the doorway of salvation. As Saint Peter declared in 1 Peter 3:18–21, "Baptism… now saves you."

In paragraphs 1262 through 1267, the *Catechism* explains these effects of baptism. They include regeneration (the rebirth in the Spirit) of the soul and the eradication of original sin as well as of actual sin and all its effects upon the soul. Through baptism we become members of the Body of Christ and are, as St. Paul says, "a new creation" in Christ (2 Corinthians 5:17), adopted sons and daughters of God. We become partakers of the divine nature, co-heirs with Christ, and temples of the Holy Spirit (1 Corinthians 3:16). Baptism serves as the sacramental doorway into the Church (Matthew 28:19).[1]

On the day of Pentecost, the people in Jerusalem who had heard Saint Peter preach called out to him, "What shall we do?" Saint Peter responded: "Repent, and be baptized every one of you in the name of Jesus Christ for the forgiveness of your sins; and you shall receive the gift of the Holy Spirit. *For the promise is to you and to your children* and to all that are far off, every one whom the Lord our God calls to him" (Acts 2:38–42, emphasis added).

Since Saint Peter was preaching to adults, he naturally told them first to repent, something necessary for any adult to do before he or she can receive baptism. Then he adds that this promise of "forgiveness of sins" and reception "of the Holy Spirit" extends to all people of all ages, "to you and to your children." The earliest Christians understood this command of baptism to include even the smallest children, who could not repent or choose baptism for themselves. Their parents brought them to be baptized, just as parents do today.

Some argue that the command to repent in Acts 2 means that repentance, something only someone above the age of reason can do (i.e., not an infant), is a prerequisite for baptism. Since infants lack the capacity to repent, they argue, infants can't be baptized. This is a faulty argument, however.

Let's apply that same logic to 2 Thessalonians 3:10, where Saint Paul says that if someone does not work he shouldn't be allowed to eat. Of course, infants cannot work. So does it follow therefore that infants should not eat? Of course not. And that insight can help us see the deeper meaning of Saint Peter's words in Acts 2. His command to "repent" can only be binding for people who have the capacity to repent. But it is not binding for those who lack that ability, such as the mentally handicapped or infants.

In the Old Testament, the outward sign of a child being brought into the covenant between God and his people was the ordinance of circumcision. This was performed on an eight-day-old boy who was brought to the temple (or synagogue) by his parents. It doesn't take a genius to figure out that eight-day-old infants don't have the capacity to understand what circumcision is and what it means—much less would a little tyke ask for circumcision, even if he did understand it! The fact is, the infant boy's parents covenanted with God on his behalf, and God accepted the child into the covenant as a result of what the parents did for the baby.

This is a helpful parallel with baptism because, after all, baptism replaced circumcision (Colossians 2:11–12). When Christian parents bring their babies to be baptized, the same thing occurs, although on the perfected, grace-filled level of a sacrament. "In the same way that a child is born into the world from the womb of his mother and has no capacity to comprehend (much less choose) what is happening to him, so, too, a child can be reborn into the life of Christ through grace and not be able to comprehend the gift of grace being bestowed on him."[2]

Mark 2:1–12 recounts the episode where Christ healed a paralyzed man. Notice that, because of his illness, the man could not approach Christ on his own. The man's friends, who wanted to see him healed, lowered him down through a hole in the roof onto the floor before Christ. "And when Jesus saw *their* faith, he said to the paralytic, 'My son, your sins are forgiven'" (emphasis added). This is another important parallel to infant baptism. God is pleased by the faith of the parents and their desire to have their child receive the graces of the sacrament of baptism.

And let's not forget what happened in Luke 18:15–17 when some disciples tried to prevent parents from bringing their children to Jesus: "Now they were bringing even infants to him that he might touch them; and when the disciples saw it, they rebuked them. But Jesus called them to him, saying, '*Let the children come to me, and do not hinder them*; for to such belongs the kingdom of God. Truly, I say to you, whoever does not receive the kingdom of God like a child shall not enter it'" (emphasis added). This passage leaves little room for doubt that Christ intends for parents to "bring even infants" to him in the sacrament of baptism.

Further Reading: Genesis 17:11; 18:16–33; Exodus 13:13–14; Leviticus 12:2–3; Matthew 8:5–13; 15:21–28; 19:13–15; Mark 16:15–16; Luke 1:59; 7:1–20; John 3:3–5, 22; Acts 16:30–33; 22:16; Romans 6:2–4; 1 Corinthians 6:11; Colossians 2:11–14; Titus 3:3–7; Hebrews 10:21–22
CCC, 535–537, 1226–1284

32

The Catholic Priesthood

Everyone knows that the Catholic Church has priests. But quite a few people (including some Catholics) don't know why. After all, some might argue, the book of Hebrews is clear that Jesus Christ is our "high priest," who offered "once for all" his perfect sacrifice on the cross for our redemption and salvation (Hebrews 7:27; 9:12, 26; 10:10). Since Christ's sacrifice was offered once for all, what need could there be for priests?

Before we consider some of the biblical evidence for the Catholic priesthood, let's first look at how the Catholic Church explains the priesthood. This special ministry of the priest is carried out in a particular way within the Church, the Body of Christ, and on its behalf.

> While the common priesthood of the faithful is exercised by the unfolding of baptismal grace—a life of faith, hope, and charity, a life according to the Spirit—the ministerial priesthood is at the service of the common priesthood.... The ministerial priesthood is a *means* by which Christ unceasingly builds up and leads his Church. For this reason it is transmitted by its own sacrament, the sacrament of Holy Orders. (CCC, 1547)

The Catholic priesthood does not in any way attempt to compete with or take the place of the unique and eternal priesthood of Jesus Christ. Rather, the Catholic priesthood *shares* in the Lord's priestly ministry.

Scripture tells us that Christ shares his sacred ministries with others. For example, Christ is the King of the universe (Mark 15:32; 1 Timothy 1:17; 6:15; Revelation 15:3; 17:14; 19:16), but his royalty is conferred on Christians, who will share in his kingship. They will wear crowns in heaven, sit on thrones, and reign as kings alongside him (Revelation 4:4, 10).

Christ is the shepherd of his flock, the Church (John 10:16), but he conferred that role, in a subordinate way, on his Apostles and on others (John 21:15–17; Ephesians 4:11). In 1 Peter 5:4, Peter calls Christ the "chief shepherd," which implies that there are lesser, subordinate shepherds.

Christ is the supreme Judge over all things (John 5:27; 9:39; Romans 14:10; 2 Corinthians 5:10; 2 Timothy 4:1), but he himself has said that Christians will also share in that judgeship, even judging the angels in heaven (Matthew 19:28; Luke 22:30; 1 Corinthians 6:2–3; Revelation 20:4).

Christ is the Creator of all that exists (John 1:1–3; Colossians 1:16–17; Hebrews 1:1–2), and he shares an aspect of his role as creator with men and women through their gift of sexual procreation.

Similarly, Jesus Christ is our "one mediator" with God, our sole "high priest" of the New Covenant," (1 Timothy 2:5; Hebrews 2:17, 3:1, 9:11) who eternally presents to the Father his redemptive sacrifice (Hebrews 3:1; 4:14–15; 5:5–10; 7:15–26; 8:1; 9:11), and he shares this priesthood.

All Christians share in the priesthood of Christ. Christians are "built into a spiritual house, to be a holy priesthood, to offer spiritual sacrifices acceptable to God through Jesus Christ"

(1 Peter 2:5–6). (See 1 Peter 2:4–9; Revelation 1:6; 5:10; 20:6.) This being the case, one might reasonably ask, "If we are all priests, why do we need priests?"

In Exodus 19:6 God told the Israelites that they were *all* priests: "You shall be to me a kingdom of priests and a holy nation" (see Isaiah 61:6). But he also made a special provision for his kingdom of priests by establishing a special *sacrificial* priesthood in their midst, as we read in Deuteronomy 33 (see Numbers 18:1–7; Malachi 1:11). Their priestly ministry prefigured the liturgical ministry of the new covenant priesthood (Matthew 28:19; John 20:23; 1 Corinthians 11:24; James 5:14).

Romans 12:4 reminds us that not every member of the body of Christ has the same function. The Catholic priesthood is a sacrificial priesthood instituted by Christ at the Last Supper, a priesthood that ministers to the "kingdom of priests" to which all baptized Christians belong. Christ perfected the imperfect ministry of the old covenant priesthood by establishing a special priestly office *within* the "kingdom of priests." To these priests he granted a special authority to offer sacrifice in his name, the sacrifice of his own Body and Blood: "Do this in remembrance of me" (Luke 22:19).

Christ's new priesthood—which is "according to the order of Melchizedek" (Psalm 110:4; Hebrews 5:6; 10:6–20)—is superior to the Aaronic priesthood in the old covenant (Hebrews 3:1–4; 7:27; 8:4–6; 9:12–14, 25; 10:5) because his once-for-all sacrifice on the cross is perfect and complete. And at every Mass, the Catholic priest follows Christ's command to "do this in memory of me." He re-presents in time and space at every Mass that once for all sacrifice of Christ.

Further Reading: Matthew 10:1, 16:16–19; 28:19; Mark 16:15; Luke 2:32; 6:13; 10:16; 24:47; John 20:22; 21:15–17;

1 Corinthians 12:28; Ephesians 4:11; 1 Thessalonians 5:12;
1 Timothy 4:14; 5:22; 2 Timothy 1:6; Titus 1:5; James 3:1
CCC, 941, 1142

33

The Divinity of Christ

Of all the doctrines of the Catholic faith, the divinity of Jesus Christ is at the very heart of everything. Our belief that the Second Person of the Blessed Trinity became a man, Jesus Christ of Galilee, some two thousand years ago, lived among us, died on the cross for our salvation and rose from the dead three days later, is known as the Incarnation.

That God himself would condescend to "take flesh" and live among us as a man is a mystery beyond our ability to fathom. But Scripture helps us penetrate at least to some depth into this august mystery, allowing us to see that Christ is true God and true man. Keeping in mind that some aggressive proselytizing groups, such as the Jehovah's Witnesses, vehemently deny the divinity of Christ and attack the faith of Catholics and other Christians who believe in this great truth, let's concentrate on several passages that reveal Christ's divinity, in order to deepen our own understanding of this doctrine and become better prepared to respond to arguments against it.

Christ's divinity was foretold in the Old Testament in passages such as Isaiah 9:6: "For to us a child is born, / to us a son is given; / and the government will be upon his shoulder, / and his name will be called / "Wonderful Counselor, *Mighty God*, / Everlasting Father, Prince of Peace" (emphasis added).

John 1:1–2, 14 says, "In the beginning was the Word, and the Word was with God, *and the Word was God*. He was in the beginning with God.... And the Word became flesh and dwelt among us, full of grace and truth; we have beheld his glory, glory as of the only Son from the Father" (emphasis added). The statement, "the Word *was* God," makes it clear that Jesus Christ was not a mere creature, neither an angel nor a super-man, but God himself. He is one divine Person who, at the Incarnation, fully possessed two natures, divine and human.

In John 1:18 we read: "No one has ever seen God; the only Son, who is in the bosom of the Father, he has made him known."

When the Apostle Thomas doubted that Christ had risen from the dead, the resurrected Christ appeared to him and invited him to probe the wounds in his hands and feet. At that, Doubting Thomas exclaimed in wonder, "My Lord and my God!" identifying Jesus as divine (John 20:28).[1]

1 Timothy 1:15–17 "Christ Jesus came into the world to save sinners. And I am the foremost of sinners; but I received mercy for this reason, that in me, as the foremost, Jesus Christ might display his perfect patience for an example to those who were to believe in him for eternal life. To the King of ages, immortal, invisible, the only God, be honor and glory for ever and ever."

Titus 2:11–14 "[We are] awaiting our blessed hope, the appearing of the glory of our great God and Savior Jesus Christ, who gave himself for us to redeem us from all iniquity and to purify for himself a people of his own who are zealous for good deeds."

Hebrews 1:5–9 "For to what angel did God ever say, / 'Thou art my Son, today I have begotten thee'? / Or again, 'I will be to him a father, and he shall be to me a son'? / And again, when he brings the first-born into the world, he says, / 'Let all God's angels *worship* him.' / Of the angels he says, 'Who makes his angels winds, and his servants flames of fire.' / But of the Son he says, / 'Thy *throne, O God, is for ever and ever*, / the righteous scepter is the scepter of thy kingdom. / Thou hast loved righteousness and hated lawlessness; / therefore God, thy God, has anointed thee / with the oil of gladness beyond thy comrades'" (emphasis added).

2 Peter 1:1 Saint Peter begins his first epistle with these words of salutation: "Simon Peter, a servant and Apostle of Jesus Christ, To those who have obtained a faith of equal standing with ours in the righteousness of our God and Savior Jesus Christ."

1 John 5:20 "And we know that the Son of God has come and has given us understanding, to know him who is true; and we are in him who is true, in *his Son Jesus Christ. This is the true God and eternal life*" (emphasis added). Notice that this reference to Jesus Christ as "the true God and eternal life" is a perfect fit with Christ's own teaching, "I am the way, and the truth, and the life" (John 14:6).

And finally, recall that when Moses encountered God in the burning bush (Exodus 3:1–22) he asked God his name. "God said to Moses, 'I AM WHO I AM.' And he said, 'Say this to the people of Israel, 'I AM has sent me to you'" (emphasis in original).

Now compare this with John 8:56–59: "'Your father Abraham rejoiced that he was to see my day; he saw it and was glad.' The Jews then said to him, 'You are not yet fifty years old, and have you seen Abraham?' Jesus said to them, 'Truly, truly, I say to you, before Abraham was, *I AM*.' So they took up stones to throw at him" (emphasis added). By saying "I AM," Jesus was declaring himself to be God. And the Jews understood this very clearly, as they sought to kill him for what they regarded as blasphemy.

In John 10:30–33 Jesus declared, "'*I and the Father are one*.' The Jews took up stones again to stone him. Jesus answered them, 'I have shown you many good works from the Father; for which of these do you stone me?' The Jews answered him, '*We stone you for no good work but for blasphemy; because you, being a man, make yourself God*'" (emphasis added).

Jesus not only claimed to be God—his audience clearly understood his meaning.

Further Reading: Compare Isaiah 43:10–12; 44:6–7 with Revelation 1:17; 2:8; 22:13. See also Romans 9:4–5; Colossians 2:9.

34

The Origin of Original Sin

Poor Saint Augustine. For quite a long time now, people have been blaming him for "inventing" the Catholic doctrine of original sin. He once wrote that the deliberate sin of Adam was the cause of original sin.[1] The fact is, however, that although Saint Augustine was the earliest Catholic writer to use the term "original sin," he was hardly the first theologian to teach that doctrine. In fact, the Bible clearly refers to original sin in several places.

To better understand the biblical evidence for original sin, let's first make sure we understand what the Catholic Church means by the term. The *Catechism* explains:

> Man, tempted by the devil, let his trust in his Creator die in his heart and, abusing his freedom, disobeyed God's command. This is what man's first sin consisted of [cf. *Gen* 3:1-11; *Rom* 5:19].... Adam and Eve immediately lose the grace of original holiness [cf. *Rom* 3:23].... The harmony in which they had found themselves, thanks to original justice, is now destroyed: the control of the soul's spiritual faculties over the body is shattered.... Finally, the consequence explicitly foretold for this disobedience will come true: man will "return to the ground" [*Gen* 3:19; cf. 2:17], for out of it he was taken. *Death makes its entrance into human history* [cf. *Rom* 5:12]. (*CCC*, 397, 399–400)

Adam and Eve's original sin wrought catastrophic consequences for all of us (cf. Genesis 2 and 3). Their original sin set the stage for our own sin, losing for themselves and for all of us those things that God had originally intended all human beings should have as safeguards against sin: control over one's passions, an enlightened intellect and grace. Scripture speaks often of this great loss to the human family:

Psalm 51:5 "Behold, I was brought forth in iniquity, / and in sin did my mother conceive me."

Wisdom of Solomon 2:23–24 "God created man for incorruption, / and made him in the image of his own eternity, / but through the devil's envy death entered the world, / and those who belong to his party experience it."

Romans 5:12 "Therefore as sin came into the world through one man and death through sin, and so death spread to all men because all men sinned."

1 Corinthians 15:21–22 "For as by a man came death, by a man has come also the resurrection of the dead. For as in Adam all die, so also in Christ shall all be made alive."

Saint Paul's statements about Adam's role in bringing "death through sin" into the world are echoes of what we read God saying to his people in Isaiah 43:27: "Your first father sinned, and your mediators transgressed against me."

Far from "inventing" original sin, the great bishop Augustine reminded us of the biblical fact that "sin came into the world through one man." And that man was Adam. However unpleasant, original sin is a reality we can face, strengthened as we are by the saving gospel of Jesus Christ through the sacrament of baptism (Acts 2:37–41; 1 Peter 3:21).

Further Reading: Wisdom of Solomon 10:1–2; Job 14:1–6;
Tobit 4:14; Sirach 10:15; John 8:44; Ephesians 2:1–4;
1 Timothy 2:13–14
CCC, 385–421

35

This Is *Your* Life!

They say that two things in life are unavoidable: death and taxes. We can add another item to that list: having all the details of our life, including our sins, completely revealed for all to see on the Last Day.

Oh joy.

The Bible repeatedly reminds us that when we are judged, individually (Hebrews 9:27) and at the general judgment (Matthew 25:31–46; Romans 2:15–16), our deeds, good and bad, and even our secret thoughts, will be made known. For most of us, that's a highly disconcerting thought.

Imagine what it must be like for a person who stands before Christ at the end of life to be judged, and has every detail of his earthly career exposed for inspection. Not a pretty picture, right? Well, there is something you can do, starting today, to make that experience much less embarrassing. The more you cultivate virtue and avoid sin, the happier your life will be *and* the less dirty laundry you'll have to be embarrassed by.

Consider these comforting words in John 3:17–21:

For God sent the Son into the world, not to condemn the world, but that the world might be saved through him. He who believes in him is not condemned; he who does not believe is condemned already, because he has not believed in the name of the only Son of God. And this is the judgment, that the light has come into the world, and men loved darkness rather than light, because their deeds were evil. For every one who does evil hates the light, and does not come to the light, lest his deeds should be exposed. But he who does what is true comes to the light, that it may be clearly seen that his deeds have been wrought in God.

That's the solution. If, when the details of your life are revealed, you have lived "in the light" of God's grace, you will have nothing to fear from his judgment. But if you have lived a life in the furtive darkness of sin, look out!

All the way back in the Garden of Eden, the truth that "you can run but you can't hide" from your sins was made clear. Genesis 3:1–13 recounts the story of how Adam and Eve ran away from their sin, attempting to hide it from God. "I was naked; and I hid myself" (v. 10).

First Corinthians 3:13 says that "each man's work will become manifest; for the Day will disclose it, because it will be revealed with fire, and the fire will test what sort of work each one has done." Verse 15 says that this process involves suffering. "He will be saved," we're told, "but only as though passing through fire." So the smart way to prepare for that day is to live a good life, frequent the sacraments, pray and avoid sin, as these passages show:

Jeremiah 23:23–24 "Am I a God at hand, says the LORD, and not a God afar off? Can a man hide himself in secret places so that I cannot see him? says the LORD. Do I not fill heaven and earth? says the LORD."

1 Corinthians 4:5 "Therefore do not pronounce judgment before the time, before the Lord comes, who will bring to light the things now hidden in darkness and will disclose the purposes of the heart. Then every man will receive his commendation from God."

Matthew 10:26   Christ said, "[N]othing is covered that will not be revealed, or hidden that will not be known."

Matthew 6:1–6   "Beware of practicing your piety before men in order to be seen by them.… But when you pray, go into your room and shut the door and pray to your Father who is in secret; and your Father who sees in secret will reward you." Here Christ reminds us that the good deeds we do in secret will also be brought to light in the end (Matthew 6:18).

Matthew 12:36–37   The Lord said, "I tell you, on the day of judgment men will render account *for every careless word they utter*; for by your words you will be justified, and by your words you will be condemned" (emphasis added). Indeed, no detail of our lives will be too small to escape notice.

Luke 12:2–3   "Beware of the leaven of the Pharisees, which is hypocrisy. Nothing is covered up that will not be revealed, or hidden that will not be known. Whatever you have said in the dark shall be heard in the light, and what you have whispered in private rooms shall be proclaimed upon the housetops."

Remember Sirach 11:27: "[A]t the close of a man's life his deeds will be revealed." We can run from our sins, but we can't hide from them. Happily, those who remain faithful to Christ won't need to do either.

Further Reading: Matthew 7:21–23; John 8:11–12; 12:44–46; Romans 2:2–15; 1 Corinthians 3:13; Ephesians 5:3–13; 2 Thessalonians 1:5–12; 2 Timothy 4:7–8

36

Reverence for Sacred Things

A few years ago, I was in Jerusalem and had the opportunity to visit the Western (or Wailing) Wall. It's all that remains visible of the massive foundation upon which the temple once stood. Several hundred Jews stood at the wall praying, bowing rhythmically as they addressed their petitions to God. The reason for this unusual motion, also known as "dovening," can be seen in passages such as 2 Chronicles 7:3 and Psalm 5:7, which speak about bowing down in fear and trembling before the presence of Almighty God.

For many, this ancient Jewish custom is utterly foreign, even weird. But in reality what's weird is not that Jews bow to show reverence at the Western Wall, but that so many Catholics have lost their sense of the sacred. They have become oblivious to those unseen holy realities that surround us.

A thoroughly secular mindset is metastasizing rapidly among Catholics and other Christians. It's common, for example, to see teens and adults come to Church on Sunday dressed in anything but their best clothes. Shorts, tank tops, flip-flop sandals, and tee shirts emblazoned with beer logos are common sights at Mass during the warmer months. What does that say to others about that person's level of reverence for Mass? What does it say to God?

Would they dress so carelessly for the prom, or if they were invited to have dinner at the White House or to a party with some celebrity? Of course not. And yet they can't be bothered to dress appropriately for the occasion of attending a banquet hosted by the King of Kings!

Irreverence for holy things takes forms other than just dressing inappropriately for Mass. There are those, for example, who visit and chitchat loudly inside the Church after Mass while others are trying to pray. That should be done in the parish hall over coffee and doughnuts, not in the presence of the Blessed Sacrament. Some people go up to receive Holy Communion while chewing gum. Others never bother to genuflect or show any form of reverence to Christ in the tabernacle.

This list of examples could be multiplied, but you get the idea. The fact is that we Catholics can learn something very important here from our Jewish friends at the Wall about respect for holy things.

Without a doubt, we need to recover our sense of the sacred, our reverence for sacred things. This holy attitude of reverence flows from what the Bible refers to as "fear of the Lord." For example, Psalm 111:10 says that "The fear of the LORD is the beginning of wisdom." (see Proverbs 1:7; 9:10).

We read in Numbers 4:15 that Aaron and his sons, the first priests who ministered to the Lord, had to wrap the liturgical vessels in cloth because those objects were so sacred that their hands were not to touch them!

Second Samuel 6:6–10 describes an astonishing episode regarding the ark of the covenant, among the most sacred artifacts in all Israel at that time. While being transported from one town to another on a cart, the oxen stumbled, causing the ark to become unstable and in danger of falling. Uzza, one of the men driving the cart, reached out to steady the ark.

Bad move.

We read that "the indignation of the LORD was enkindled against [Uzza], and he struck him for his rashness: and he died there before the ark of God" (DR). That's a pretty clear indication that God wants people to exercise respect for sacred things.

In Exodus 3:1–5 we read about how the very *ground* on which Moses stood was considered sacred because it was in the immediate presence of God as he appeared in the burning bush.

Consider these other passages that speak about the importance of reverence for sacred things.

Leviticus 19:30 "God commanded, 'You shall…reverence my sanctuary'" (see Leviticus 26:2).

Psalm 5:7 "I will come into thy house; I will worship towards thy holy temple, in thy fear" (literally, in "awe" of thee) (DR).

Matthew 7:6 "Give not that which is holy to dogs; neither cast ye your pearls before swine, lest perhaps they trample them under their feet, and turning upon you, they tear you" (DR).

Hebrews 12:28 "Therefore let us be grateful for receiving a kingdom that cannot be shaken, and thus let us offer to God acceptable worship, with reverence and awe; for our God is a consuming fire" (see Hebrews 10:31).

Further Reading: Deuteronomy 32:51; 2 Chronicles 19:7–9; Job 28:28; Proverbs 15:16, 33; 22:4; Psalm 19:9; 34:11; Isaiah 11:2–3; 2 Corinthians 5:11; Ephesians 5:21

37

Don't Delay Conversion!

You've heard the saying, "When you least expect it, expect it." Consider those words in light of the horror of the tsunami that devastated Southeast Asia on December 26, 2004, killing some 200,000 people. Many of those killed were relaxing on the beach one moment, and the next, being swept away to their deaths. One moment, they were having fun, the next moment they found themselves standing before Christ the Judge, having to render to him an account of their lives. "[I]t is appointed for men to die once, and after that comes judgment" (Hebrews 9:27).

How many of those tsunami victims were prepared for their eternal judgment? How prepared would *you* be if your life ended suddenly?

The tsunami tragedy is a grim but important reminder that we must always be spiritually prepared to die. This means a sincere conversion of heart, repentance and turning away from sin and a return to the sacraments. Since we have no way of knowing when death will come, the only sane option is to live in such a way that we are always ready.

In his classic work *The Imitation of Christ*, Thomas à Kempis wrote: "Every action of yours, every thought, should be those of one who expects to die before the day is out. Death would have no great terrors for you if you had a quiet conscience.... Then why not keep clear of sin instead of running away from death? If you aren't fit to face death today, it's very unlikely you will be tomorrow."[1]

These Scripture passages make this point perfectly clear:

Isaiah 55:6–7 "Seek the LORD while he may be found, / call upon him while he is near; / let the wicked forsake his way, / and the unrighteous man his thoughts; / let him return to the LORD, that he may have mercy on him, / and to our God, for he will abundantly pardon."

James 4:13–15 "Come now, you who say, 'Today or tomorrow we will go into such and such a town and spend a year there and trade and get gain'; whereas you do not know about tomorrow. What is your life? For you are a mist that appears for a little time and then vanishes. Instead you ought to say, 'If the Lord wills, we shall live and we shall do this or that.'"

Luke 12:16–21 "The land of a rich man brought forth plentifully; and he thought to himself, 'What shall I do, for I have nowhere to store my crops?' And he said, 'I will do this: I will pull down my barns, and build larger ones; and there I will store all my grain and my goods. And I will say to my soul, Soul, you have ample goods laid up for many years; take your ease, eat, drink, be merry.' But God said to him, 'Fool! This night your soul is required of you; and the things you have prepared, whose will they be?' So is he who lays up treasure for himself, and is not rich toward God."

Matthew 25:1–13 "Then the kingdom of heaven shall be compared to ten maidens who took their lamps and went to meet the bridegroom. Five of them were foolish, and five were wise. For when the foolish took their lamps, they took no oil with them; but the wise took flasks of oil with their lamps. As the bridegroom was delayed, they all slumbered and slept. But at midnight there was a cry, 'Behold, the bridegroom! Come out to meet him.' Then all those maidens rose and trimmed their lamps. And the foolish said to the wise, 'Give us some of your oil, for our lamps are going out.' But the wise replied, 'Perhaps there will not be enough for us and for you; go rather to the dealers and buy for yourselves.' And while they went to buy, the bridegroom came, and those who were ready went in with him to the marriage feast; and the door was shut. Afterward the other maidens came also, saying, 'Lord, lord, open to us.' But he replied, 'Truly, I say to you, I do not know you.' Watch therefore, for you know neither the day nor the hour."

Mark 13:32–37 "Take heed, watch and pray; for you do not know when the time will come. It is like a man going on a journey, when he leaves home and puts his servants in charge, each with his work, and commands the doorkeeper to be on the watch. Watch therefore—for you do not know when the master of the house will come, in the evening, or at midnight, or at cockcrow, or in the morning—lest he come suddenly and find you asleep. And what I say to you I say to all: Watch."

1 Thessalonians 5:2–6 "For you yourselves know well that the day of the Lord will come like a thief in the night. When people say, 'There is peace and security,' then sudden destruction will come upon them as travail [i.e., labor pains] comes upon a woman with child, and there will be no escape. But you are not in darkness, brethren, for that day to surprise you like a thief."

Sirach 5:7 "Do not delay to turn to the Lord, / nor postpone it from day to day; / for suddenly the wrath of the Lord will go forth, / and at the time of punishment you will perish."

Saint Francis of Assisi wrote, "Praised are you, my Lord, for our sister bodily death, from whom no living man can escape. Woe on those who will die in mortal sin! Blessed are they who will be found in your most holy will, for the second death will not harm them."[2] He understood the importance of preparing for death, and that the most foolish thing one can do is delay his conversion. Some people, sadly, delay too long—and by then it's too late.

Further Reading: Genesis 3:19; Deuteronomy 32:29; Job 14:5; Sirach 1:13; Ecclesiastes 7:1–2, 11:8; Psalm 103:15–16; Matthew 24:48–51; Luke 12:35–37; 21:36; Hebrews 10:31; 1 Peter 4:7; Revelation 3:2–3
CCC, 1005–1060

38

The Myth of a "Total Apostasy"

You've seen them riding through your neighborhood in pairs on bicycles. Mormon missionaries, clean-cut young men wearing white shirts, dark trousers and conservative ties, show up every day on thousands of doorsteps just like yours, intent on making converts to the Church of Jesus Christ of Latter-day Saints— commonly known as the Mormon Church.

One of Mormonism's main tenets is that their church is the "restored" church, a "restoration of the gospel" by their founder, Joseph Smith, Jr., in 1830. They believe that this "restoration" was necessary due to a complete falling away or "total apostasy" of the true Church established by Jesus Christ in Palestine. It's an interesting theory, but it's completely false.

One of the former general authorities of the Mormon Church wrote: "This universal apostasy began in the days of the ancient Apostles themselves; and it was known to and foretold by them.... With the loss of the Gospel, the nations of the earth went into a moral eclipse called the Dark Ages. Apostasy was universal.... [T]his darkness still prevails except among those who have come to a knowledge of the restored Gospel."[1]

Wrong.

Mormonism's total apostasy argument collapses when tested against the facts of Scripture and Church history. If the alleged "total apostasy" of the Church had actually happened, Christ himself would have been a liar when he promised: "[O]n this rock I will build my church, and the gates of hell shall not prevail against it (Matthew 16:18, DR).

True, the Bible does mention an apostasy in passages such as Matthew 24:4–12, Mark 13:21–23, Luke 21:7–8, Acts 20:29–30, 2 Thessalonians 2:1–12, 2 Timothy 3:1–7, 2 Timothy 4:3–4, 2 Peter 2:1–3 and Jude 1:17–19. Some of these verses say "many" will fall away, but not a single one says *all* will fall away. Also, these passages speak about these apostasies occurring during the "end times," or the "latter days," as the King James Bible renders it. Even Mormons will admit that the second or third centuries (when they think a total apostasy happened) were not the "latter days."

Scripture is clear: The Church Christ established is indefectible because Christ, God himself, is unconquerable. He promised to be with his Church "even until the end of the world" (see Matthew 28:20).

In Matthew 7:24–29 Christ said that a "wise man" is the one who "built his house upon a rock." It cannot be overcome or overwhelmed by anything. And recall that in Matthew 16:18 he promised Simon Peter, "[O]n this rock I will build my church, and the powers of death shall not prevail against it." Surely, he would not tell us to do something that he himself was incapable of doing.

In Matthew 12:29 Christ speaks of a "strong man" guarding his house. Unless an enemy can "bind" the strong man, the enemy cannot enter and plunder the house. Then in 1 Timothy 3:15 we read that the *Church* is Christ's house. Obviously, Christ is stronger than Satan; and so Satan could not plunder Christ's Church through apostasy unless he first bound Christ, the Strong Man. This means that there has not been, and can never be, a total apostasy of the Church, as Mormons erroneously claim. For if it were possible, then Christ was either a liar for promising his permanent protection to the Church (Luke 14:27–30, Matthew 28:20), or a fool for making promises he couldn't keep.

Scripture clearly evidences that Christ's Church cannot be overcome. Isaiah 9:6–7 prophesies Christ upholding his kingdom "for evermore": "For to us a child is born, / to us a son is given; / and the government will be upon his shoulder, / and his name will be called / 'Wonderful Counselor, Mighty God, / Everlasting Father, / Prince of Peace.' *Of the increase of his government and of peace / there will be no end, / upon the throne of David, and over his kingdom, / to establish it, and to uphold it / with justice and with righteousness / from this time forth and for evermore*" (emphasis added).

Nothing will bring down Christ's kingdom; there will never be a time when he lets it slip or fall. If the Church fell into total apostasy a few generations after Christ's Ascension, then he did not uphold his kingdom, as Scripture promises he will.

Similarly, Daniel 2:44 says, "And in the days of those kings the God of heaven will set up a kingdom *which shall never be destroyed*, nor shall its sovereignty be left to another people. It shall break in pieces all these kingdoms and bring them to an end, and *it shall stand for ever*" (emphasis added).

Here, Daniel prophesies five kingdoms: the Babylonian, the Median, the Persian, the Greek and the kingdom of God, that is, the Church. Notice that the final kingdom will "never be destroyed" and shall "stand for ever." This prophecy could not be true if the Church had indeed collapsed into a complete apostasy and had to be restored fifteen or sixteen centuries later.

Daniel 7:14 says, "And to him was given dominion / and glory and kingdom, / that all peoples, nations, and languages / should serve him; / his dominion is an everlasting dominion, / which shall not pass away, / *and his kingdom one / that shall not be destroyed*"(emphasis added). Here again, this prophecy shows apostasy cannot overcome Christ's kingdom, the Church.

One final example of how Scripture disproves the Mormon theory of a total apostasy is found in Luke 1:30–33: "And the angel said to her, 'Do not be afraid, Mary, for you have found favor with God. And behold, you will conceive in your womb and bear a son, and you shall call his name Jesus. He will be great, and will be called the Son of the Most High; / and the Lord God will give to him the throne of his father David, / and he will reign over the house of Jacob for ever; / *and of his kingdom there will be no end*'" (emphasis added).

Further Reading: Isaiah 9:6–7; Daniel 2:11–15; 7:13–14; Matthew 7:24–29; 12:29; 28:18–20; Mark 3:27; Luke 1:30–33; 14:27–30; John 14:15–20; 1 Corinthians 11:26; 2 Timothy 4:2–4; 2 Peter 2:1–2; Revelation 13:7

39

The Field of Wheat and Weeds

On one occasion, Jesus put this parable before the crowd gathered around him:

> The kingdom of heaven may be compared to a man who sowed good seed in his field; but while men were sleeping, his enemy came and sowed weeds among the wheat, and went away. So when the plants came up and bore grain, then the weeds appeared also. And the servants of the householder came and said to him, "Sir, did you not sow good seed in your field? How then has it weeds?" He said to them, "An enemy has done this." The servants said to him, "Then do you want us to go and gather them?" But he said, "No; lest in gathering the weeds you root up the wheat along with them. Let both grow together until the harvest; and at harvest time I will tell the reapers, Gather the weeds first and bind them in bundles to be burned, but gather the wheat into my barn." (Matthew 13:24–30)

In this age of scandals in the Church, these words of Christ should reassure us. They are a reminder that, from the very beginning, the Church (the "kingdom of heaven") has been comprised of "wheat and weeds," good and bad, saints and sinners, and everyone in between.

For the two thousand years that the Catholic Church has been in existence, it's always been this way. At times, there may seem to be more weeds than wheat in the Church, but each generation can take consolation that in spite of bad Catholics—priests and bishops, as well as lay people— Jesus Christ is in charge. The Catholic Church is *his* Church, not ours, and it remains what it has ever been: a field of wheat and weeds.

Saint Thomas Aquinas commented on this reality in his *Summa Theologica*: "To be 'a glorious Church, not having spot or wrinkle' [Ephesians 5:27] is the ultimate end to which we are brought by the Passion of Christ. Hence this will be in heaven, and not on earth, in which 'if we say we have no sin, we deceive ourselves,' as it is written" [1 John 1:8].[1] We know that the Church and all its faithful members will eventually be purified and become the "spotless" bride of Christ (Revelation 19:7; 21:2–17), but in the meantime, the process of purification reminds us that there is much to be purified from.

Sometimes we can become discouraged in the face of scandals. Some are even tempted to abandon ship out of an understandable, though misguided, assumption that the Catholic Church cannot possibly be the true Church, given that there are so many sinful Catholics—especially when the details of these sometimes spectacular moral failings end up splashed across the front page of the newspaper. But as understandable as it is, the "abandon ship" mentality is exactly the opposite of how a Catholic should feel in the face of scandals.

First, we should recognize that our own hearts are microcosms of the Church. Each of us is a complicated mix of saint and sinner. We each have a field of wheat and weeds, virtue and sin, love for God and rebellion against him, present within us. Is it not true that your heart, like mine, has a few weeds—perhaps more than a few—flourishing in those darker recesses?

The weeds of greed, anger, gluttony, lust for sexual pleasure, deceit, hard-heartedness, gossip, laziness, drunkenness, covetousness, pride and the like are present in the hearts of many Catholics. Is it not true, then, that before we bemoan the weeds that exist in the Church, we should first attend to the weeds in our own souls?

The second reason we should never be tempted to abandon ship is that, no matter how difficult or even hopeless things in the Church may appear (and never forget that appearances are often deceiving), Jesus Christ is always true to his word. He will not let the Church be overcome by the storms of sin and temptation. No matter what.

Consider the time when Christ and the Apostles were in a boat on Lake Galilee. "But he was in the stern, asleep on the cushion; and they woke him and said to him, 'Teacher, do you not care if we perish?' And he awoke and rebuked the wind, and said to the sea, 'Peace! Be still!' And the wind ceased, and there was a great calm. He said to them, 'Why are you afraid? Have you no faith?'" (Mark 4:35–41).

The Apostles' complaint, "Do you not care if we perish?" is echoed in the hearts of some Catholics today, discouraged and demoralized as they are by scandals. They worry that perhaps Christ has fallen asleep on the job, or has lost interest in the Church. Neither is true, of course.

Jesus Christ "remains faithful," as Saint Paul reminds us in 2 Timothy 2:11–15. He will not abandon his Church: "[B]ehold, I am with you all days, even till the consummation of the world" (Matthew 28:20, DR). The Lord promised, "I will not leave you orphans" (John 14:18, DR). You can trust these promises Christ made. He made them to you and to me every bit as much as he did to the Apostles.

The next time you or someone you know is tempted to discouragement when the latest scandal involving a Catholic hits the news, just remember the Lord's promise: "I have said this to you, that in me you may have peace. In the world you have tribulation; but be of good cheer, I have overcome the world" (John 16:33).

Yes, the Catholic Church, like our own hearts, is truly a field of wheat and weeds, and it will be until the end. But in the meantime, Christ wants to give us the graces we need to deal with those weeds. All we have to do is ask him (Matthew 11:28).

40

Lust and Impurity

As a young man, Aurelius Augustinus was no saint. In later years, though, he became a renowned theologian and the holy bishop of Hippo, North Africa. We know him today as *Saint Augustine*, for so he became. But in his youth, sanctity was the last thing on his mind.

Before experiencing a radical conversion to Jesus Christ in his early thirties, Augustine was, to put it simply, addicted to sexual pleasure. He admitted this freely in his famous autobiography *Confessions*, which recounts with painful honesty the details of his sins and the consequences they wreaked on his life. But as he experienced so powerfully, God's grace is more powerful than man's sin.

The arc of Saint Augustine's life—his loss of innocence, his descent into chronic sexual sin, his gradual struggle to free himself, his eventual liberation by God's grace and his wholehearted embrace of virtue, especially chastity—teaches us a great deal. Many, many people these days, including many Catholics, find themselves in the grip of lust and various forms of impurity and unchastity. Many wonder if they can ever break free from their addictions. The allure of lust is so powerful, so seductive, that even Christians who know consenting to lust is wrong suffer pangs of hesitancy, as did Augustine, who once prayed in a moment of temptation: "Give me chastity...but not yet!"[1]

To make matters worse, virtually every level of modern media contributes to this problem. Eroticism and pornography flood our modern culture with the incessant message that hedonism and unlimited gratification is good, and that, conversely, self-restraint, chastity and modesty are, if not bad, at least weird.

But Scripture tells us otherwise. In Matthew 5:27–30 the Lord warns,

> You have heard that it was said, "You shall not commit adultery." But I say to you that *every one who looks at a woman lustfully has already committed adultery with her in his heart*. If your right eye causes you to sin, pluck it out and throw it away; it is better that you lose one of your members than that your whole body be thrown into hell. And if your right hand causes you to sin, cut it off and throw it away; it is better that you lose one of your members than that your whole body go into hell (Matthew 5:28, emphasis added; see Matthew 15:19; Mark 7:21).

In Romans 13:14 Saint Paul says, "[P]ut on the Lord Jesus Christ, and make no provision for the flesh, to gratify its desires." This is a reminder that the old saying is true: Give the devil an inch and he'll take a mile. In other words, a seemingly minor concession to impurity can quickly snowball out of control and will cascade into serious sin. Just ask any priest who's been hearing confessions for awhile.

Happily, the Lord provides the grace to withstand temptations toward lust and impurity, as well as the grace of forgiveness and restoration for those who repent. We have only to ask him. In John 8:1–11 we see the incident of the woman caught in adultery. Her accusers were about to stone her to death when Christ intervened, dispersing the rock-throwers with a single statement, "Let him who is without sin among you be the first to throw a stone at her" (v. 7). He forgave the weeping woman, saying, "'Woman, where are they? Has no one condemned you?' She said, 'No one, Lord.' And Jesus said, 'Neither do I condemn you; *go, and do not sin again*'" (emphasis added).

Consider these other warnings about lust, impurity and unchastity:

1 Corinthians 6:9–11 "Do you not know that the unrighteous will not inherit the kingdom of God? Do not be deceived; neither the immoral, nor idolaters, nor adulterers, nor homosexuals, nor thieves, nor the greedy, nor drunkards, nor revilers, nor robbers will inherit the kingdom of God. And such were some of you. But you were washed, you were sanctified, you were justified in the name of the Lord Jesus Christ and in the Spirit of our God."

1 Corinthians 6:13–20 "The body is not meant for immorality, but for the Lord, and the Lord for the body.... Do you not know that your bodies are members of Christ? Shall I therefore take the members of Christ and make them members of a prostitute? Never! Do you not know that he who joins himself to a prostitute becomes one body with her? For, as it is written, 'The two shall become one.' But he who is united to the Lord becomes one spirit with him. Shun immorality. Every other sin which a man commits is outside the body; but the immoral man sins against his own body. Do you not know that your body is a temple of the Holy Spirit within you, which you have from God? You are not your own; you were bought with a price. So glorify God in your body."

Colossians 3:5–8 "Put to death therefore what is earthly in you: immorality, impurity, passion, evil desire, and covetousness, which is idolatry. On account of these the wrath of God is coming. In these you once walked, when you lived in them. But now put them all away: anger, wrath, malice, slander, and foul talk from your mouth."

1 Thessalonians 4:3–7 "For this is the will of God, your sanctification: that you abstain from immorality; that each one of you know how to control his own body in holiness and honor, not in the passion of lust like heathen who do not know God; that no man transgress, and wrong his brother in this matter, because the Lord is an avenger in all these things, as we solemnly forewarned you. For God has not called us for uncleanness, but in holiness."

2 Peter 2:9–10 "[T]he Lord knows how to rescue the godly from trial, and to keep the unrighteous under punishment until the day of judgment, and *especially those who indulge in the lust of defiling passion and despise authority*" (emphasis added).

1 John 2:15–17 "Do not love the world or the things in the world. If any one loves the world, love for the Father is not in him. For all that is in the world, the lust of the flesh and the lust of the eyes and the pride of life, is not of the Father but is of the world. And the world passes away, and the lust of it; but he who does the will of God abides for ever."

One final point: The word "pornography" comes from the Greek word *porneia*, which means sexual unlawfulness or immorality. Several passages in the New Testament warn about the danger of *porneia*, whether it involves physical sins of the flesh (adultery, fornication, masturbation and so on) or sins of the mind (deliberately viewing pornography, lusting in one's heart after others, and the like).

First Thessalonians 4:3 (cited above) says to "abstain from…immorality [*porneia*]." In 1 Corinthians 6:18 Saint Paul says "shun immorality [*porneia*]." Likewise, Ephesians 5:3 says that "immorality and all impurity [*porneia*] or covetousness must not even be named among you."

Further Reading: CCC, 2331–2400, 2514–2533

41

The Sacraments

Those of us who are old enough to remember learning our catechism lessons from the venerable *Baltimore Catechism* will know by heart the answer to question 136: "What is a Sacrament?"

"*A sacrament is an outward sign instituted by Christ to give grace.*" Those twelve words are a succinct explanation of what the sacraments are, what they do and where they come from.

Let's consider what an outward sign is. By its very nature, an outward sign is something physical and material. To draw an imperfect but still useful parallel, the outward sign of who you are is your body. What others can see of you is not your soul (which is pure spirit and therefore unable to be perceived by one's bodily senses) but your body, which is the outward, visible part of you.

We know many things around us by the means of signs. A flashing red light is a sign warning of some danger in the vicinity. The smell of alcohol on a motorist's breath is a sign that he's been drinking and may be driving while intoxicated. The black robe worn by a Supreme Court justice is a sign of his or her office. An airline pilot's uniform is a sign that he is qualified to fly the plane. Although a married woman's wedding ring isn't itself a sacrament (rather, it's a sacrament*al*), it is an outward sign that points toward an unseen, inward reality—her physical and spiritual union with her husband.

Since sacraments are instituted by Christ, it follows that the Church does not—indeed, it *cannot*—create or reconfigure a sacrament. Each of the seven sacraments (baptism, confession, the Holy Eucharist, confirmation, matrimony, holy orders, and anointing of the sick) has its source in Jesus Christ, who alone established them as means of grace for his Church.

Also, the sacraments "give grace." This means that a validly celebrated sacrament instills a special spiritual benefit in the soul. In the sacrament of baptism, for example, original sin is eliminated and all actual sin (mortal or venial) is eradicated, as are all temporal effects due to sin. The baptized person is regenerated and justified in God's grace, becoming his adopted son or daughter; sanctifying grace, which is the very life of the Blessed Trinity, is infused into the person's soul.

The essential *outward sign* of these spectacular spiritual realities is the combination of the pouring of the baptismal water and the pronouncing of the words of the sacrament: "I baptize you in the name of the Father, and of the Son and of the Holy Spirit." (Immersion is also valid for baptism.)

Let's examine some key Bible passages in which the seven sacraments appear. In some cases we see Christ directly commanding them; in others we see the New Testament writers teaching about them.

BAPTISM

Christ commands baptism in Matthew 28:19 and speaks of its necessity in Mark 16:15 and John 3:3–5; Saint Paul says that baptism is the means by which Christ sanctifies the Church and cleanses those baptized by the "bath of regeneration" in Titus 3:5; and Saint Peter describes the effects of baptismal regeneration in

Acts 2:37–39 (see Ezekiel 36:25; Matthew 3:13; John 4:2; 1 Corinthians 6:11; Ephesians 5:26).

Confession (Penance)

The Bible contains numerous warnings about the necessity of repenting from sin and doing penance, as part of the Lord's plan of salvation for those who love him (Ezekiel 18:30; 33:11; Jeremiah 18:11; 25:5; Joel 2:12; Matthew 3:2; 4:7; Acts 2:38). In John 20:20–23 Christ gives his Apostles the authority to forgive sins. In 2 Corinthians 5:18–20 Saint Paul emphasizes the "ministry of reconciliation" that he and the other Apostles had received from Christ. And Christ gave to Peter and the other Apostles (and through them, to their successors) the authority to "bind and loose" (Matthew 16:19; 18:18), promising them that "He who hears you hears me" (Luke 10:16). This authority to "bind and loose" includes the forgiveness of sins through the sacrament of confession.

The Holy Eucharist

Christ foretells the institution of this most holy sacrament of his Body and Blood in John 6:22–65. At the Last Supper he formally institutes it during the first Mass (Matthew 26:26–28; Mark 14:22–34; Luke 22:15–20; 1 Corinthians 11:23–29; see also Genesis 14:18; Psalm 110:1–4; Malachi 1:11; Hebrews 5:6; 7:1).

Confirmation

Christ promises the Church the "gift of the Holy Spirit" in passages such as Luke 24:49, John 7:38; 14:16, 26; 16:7 and Acts 1:5. In Acts 2:4 we see the first confirmation when the Holy Spirit came upon the Apostles under the *outward sign* of tongues of fire. After this, the imposition of hands of the bishop (or his representative) and the anointing with oil served as the outward sign of confirmation (Acts 8:14–17). In Acts 19:6 we see Saint Paul confirm a dozen of his newly baptized followers by laying hands on them, as a result of which they received the gift of the Holy Spirit in a new and unique way (see Hebrews 6:2).

HOLY MATRIMONY

The sacramental union of a man and a woman signifies the insoluble spousal union between Christ and the Church (Ephesians 5:21–32). It finds its origin in the Garden of Eden, where God united Adam and Eve and commanded them to "[b]e fruitful and multiply" (Genesis 1:26–28; 2:18–25). Jesus Christ, present in utero at the wedding of his Mother, the Blessed Virgin Mary, and his stepfather, Saint Joseph (Matthew 1:18–25; Luke 2:3–5), sanctified and elevated the Old Testament ordinance of marriage to a new and supernatural level, as did his presence at the wedding at Cana (John 2:1–11).

HOLY ORDERS

Christ conferred the sacrament of holy orders (that is, ordination to the priesthood) upon the Twelve Apostles at the Last Supper (Matthew 26:26 28; Mark 14.22–24, Luke 22.15–20) when he simultaneously instituted the sacrament of the Holy Eucharist. His words "Do this in remembrance of me" indicate the sacrificial nature of this new priesthood, which is not temporary and ineffectual as was the Jewish Levitical priesthood of the Old Testament (Hebrews 10:1–18). Rather, the new priesthood is permanent and effective because it shares in Christ's own unique priesthood (Hebrews 9:11–14, 23–28). Acts 1:15–26 reveals the ordination of the first bishop, Matthias, who replaced Judas Iscariot. Passages such as Acts 6:6 and 14:22, as well 1 Timothy 4:14 and 5:22, show us that the Apostles and their successors ordained bishops, priests (*presbyters*) and deacons, which are the three levels of holy orders.

ANOINTING OF THE SICK

This sacrament is first glimpsed in Mark 6:7–13, where Christ commissions his Apostles to heal the sick and cast out demons through the use of prayer and anointing. James 5:13–15 explicitly prescribes that the afflicted seek the sacrament of anointing (see 1 Corinthians 12:9).

Further Reading: CCC, 1113–1134, 1135–1666

42

Apostolic Succession

When a man is ordained a bishop in the Catholic Church, he becomes a living link in the two thousand-year-old chain of apostolic succession, which stretches unbroken from Jesus Christ to our present day. He receives a unique share in the authority and duties of the original twelve Apostles, and he becomes part of the living *magisterium*—the teaching office of the Church that is entrusted with the task of authentically proclaiming, explaining and defending the deposit of faith that was "once for all delivered to the saints" (Jude 3).

The Apostles understood that after their own deaths, their ministry would need to continue as a permanent, living presence with the Church "until the end of the age" (Matthew 28:20, NRSV) when Christ the Lord would return. As such, we see that early on they made provisions for this handing on of their ministry to men whom they knew were worthy of the task entrusted to them (see CCC 3, 860–862, 1576).

The following biblical passages reveal that apostolic succession—the handing on of the apostolic office of "overseer" down through the ages—is not some Catholic invention but is precisely what the Apostles practiced and taught.

In Acts 1:15–26 we see the first glimpse of apostolic succession. Judas Iscariot, one of the original twelve Apostles, had not only betrayed the Lord but he then fell into despair and committed suicide. This left a vacancy in the college of Apostles—they needed a replacement.

Peter, after lamenting Judas's actions, spoke to the brethren assembled for the election: "[I]t is written in the book of Psalms, 'Let his habitation become desolate, / and let there be no one to live in it'; and / '*His office let another take*' [Greek: "let his *episkopen* (bishopric) be taken up by another"].…. And they prayed and said, 'Lord, who knowest the hearts of all men, show which one of these two thou hast chosen to take the place in this ministry and apostleship from which Judas turned aside, to go to his own place.' And they cast lots for them, and the lot fell on Matthias; and he was enrolled with the eleven apostles."

Accompanying Christ during his public ministry was a requirement for this first man to stand in the line of apostolic succession, but this prerequisite quickly fell away.

In Acts 20:28 Saint Paul reminds certain elders in Ephesus that they are "overseers" who have the special task of caring for the Church. The Greek word he uses for "overseers" is *episcopous*, which literally means "bishops." *Episcopos* (bishop) derives from two words *epi*, which means "over" or "above," and *skopéo*, which means "to look."

First Thessalonians 1:1–20 reveals the new role as bishop of two protégés of Saint Paul, Timothy and Silvanus. The opening of this epistle reads: "Paul, Silvanus, and Timothy, To the church of the Thessalonians in God the Father and the Lord Jesus Christ…" The rest of the epistle is written with the pronouns "we," "us" and "our," which indicates that Saint Paul regarded Timothy and Silvanus as his fellow Apostles who had the authority to teach the Thessalonians. This fact becomes clear in chapter 2, verse 6, where he reminds them that "*we* might have made demands as apostles of Christ" (emphasis added). While it's true that all Christians are literally "apostles" (Greek: "one who is sent") by virtue of baptism, the context of this passage implies the office of an Apostle in a particular sense. Saint Paul meant his audience to understand that Timothy and Silvanus also exercised apostolic authority in a special way (2 Timothy 1:6).

Paul wrote to Titus (1:5–9):

> This is why I left you in Crete, that you might amend what was defective, and appoint elders in every town as I directed you, if any man is blameless, the husband of one wife, and his children are believers and not open to the charge of being profligate or insubordinate. For a bishop, as God's steward, must be blameless; he must not be arrogant or quick-tempered or a drunkard or violent or greedy for gain, but hospitable, a lover of goodness, master of himself, upright, holy, and self-controlled; he must hold firm to the sure word as taught, so that he may be able to give instruction in sound doctrine and also to confute those who contradict it.

In 1 Timothy 4:14 and 2 Timothy 1:6 Saint Paul reminds Timothy, a young bishop, of his ordination by the "laying on of hands," and in 1 Timothy 3:1–7, he explains the qualifications for a worthy candidate for bishop. In 1 Timothy 5:22 Saint Paul advises Timothy, "Do not be hasty in the laying on of hands" (that is, ordaining others to the priesthood and episcopacy).

First Corinthians 12:27–29 mentions various duties in the early Church; Paul lists the foremost among them as "Apostles." These are the bishops who stand in the line of apostolic succession from the original twelve. Ephesians 4:11–12 echoes this theme, and Ephesians 2:19–20 adds that the "household of God [is] built upon the foundation of the apostles and prophets, Christ Jesus himself being the cornerstone."

Second Timothy 2:1–2 is yet another example of apostolic

succession in action in the early Church. Saint Paul writes, "You then, my son, be strong in the grace that is in Christ Jesus, and what you have heard from me before many witnesses entrust to faithful men who will be able to teach others also." We see here that Saint Paul, who was made an Apostle by Christ, had ordained Timothy to the office of bishop; he in turn exhorts Timothy to be careful to whom he entrusts the message of the gospel. He was to choose wisely, in order that those whom he ordained to be bishops would, in their turn, also choose well the men to whom they would entrust the teachings of the Church.

Each time a man is ordained a bishop, he receives what Saint Paul entrusted to Timothy, what Timothy entrusted to the bishops he ordained and what all bishops down through the centuries have received and passed down: the apostolic office of the episcopacy.

43

The "Brothers" of the Lord

The Catholic Church teaches that the Blessed Virgin Mary remained a virgin throughout her life, before and after the birth of Christ. "The Virgin Birth" refers to the fact that Christ was conceived in Mary's womb without the involvement of a human father (Saint Joseph being his foster father). Another aspect of this teaching is known as "the Perpetual Virginity of Mary," meaning that she did not bear other children besides her son, Jesus.

How then do we account for certain passages in Scripture that speak of the "brothers of the Lord"? Do they contradict Catholic teaching and indicate that Mary did, in fact, have other children after she gave birth to Jesus?

Not at all.

In any explicit sense, the New Testament is completely silent in regard to whether or not Mary had other children besides Christ. It also does not explicitly state that she remained a virgin after his birth. But the *implicit* evidence that she remained a perpetual virgin is considerable.

First, keep in mind that in Hebrew, Aramaic and Greek, the term "brother" in the time of Christ denoted any close male relative or friend. Uncles, nephews and cousins were routinely called brother in the Jewish culture of the time of the Lord and for centuries before.

In passages such as Genesis 13:8, we see that Lot was the nephew of Abraham, though he is called Abraham's "brother."[1] Passages such as Deuteronomy 23:8, Nehemiah 5:7, 2 Kings 10:13–14, Jeremiah 34:9, 2 Samuel 1:26, 1 Kings 9:11–13 and 1 Kings 20:32 show this usage to have been very common.

In Matthew 12:46–50, Mark 3:31–35 and Mark 6:3, certain men were called the "brothers" of the Lord. Matthew 13:55 says: "Is not this the carpenter's son? Is not his mother called Mary? And are not his brethren James and Joseph and Simon and Judas?" (that is, Jude Thaddeus, not Judas Iscariot).

Two of these four men called "brothers," James and Joseph, must have been close relatives of Jesus, but they definitely were not the sons of Mary his mother. The same is true for Judas (Jude) who was the son of another woman. How do we know this? Because the Bible tells us that the first two men were the sons of Mary the wife of Alphaeus [also Cleophas or Clopas], who was either the sister or cousin or some other close relation to Mary the mother of Jesus.

Matthew 10:2–3 "The names of the twelve Apostles are these: first, Simon, who is called Peter, and Andrew his brother; James the son of Zebedee, and John his brother; Philip and Bartholomew; Thomas and Matthew the tax collector; *James the son of Alphaeus*, and Thaddaeus; Simon the Cananaean, and Judas Iscariot, who betrayed him" (emphasis added).

Matthew 27:55–56 "There were also many women there [at the foot of the cross], looking on from afar, who had followed Jesus from Galilee, ministering to him; among whom were Mary Magdalene, *and Mary the mother of James and Joseph*, and the mother of the sons of Zebedee" (emphasis added).

Mark 15:40 "There were also women looking on from afar [from the foot of the cross], among whom were Mary Magdalene, *and*

Mary the mother of James the younger and of Joses [i.e., Joseph], *and Salome*, who, when he was in Galilee, followed him, and ministered to him; and also many other women who came up with him to Jerusalem" (emphasis added).

Luke 6:13–16 "And when it was day, he called his disciples, and chose from them twelve, whom he named apostles; Simon, whom he named Peter, and Andrew his brother, and James and John, and Philip, and Bartholomew, and Matthew, and Thomas, *and James the son of Alphaeus*, and Simon who was called the Zealot, *and Judas the son of James*, and Judas Iscariot, who became a traitor" (emphasis added).

John 19:25 "[S]tanding by the cross of Jesus were his mother, and his mother's sister, Mary the wife of Clopas, and Mary Magdalene."

The preceding passages are sufficient to dispel the notion that the men mentioned in Matthew 13 were the literal brothers of Jesus, sons of Mary his mother. They were not. These men were the Lord's first cousins or perhaps some other close kin. Those early Church Fathers who commented on these passages tell us that Cleophas was Saint Joseph's brother, which would make his sons James and Joses (assuming that Cleophas and Clopas were the same man), the cousins of the Lord.

Additional clues also point us toward the truth of Mary's perpetual virginity. For example, of the scene of the Crucifixion, we read: "When Jesus saw his mother, and the disciple whom he loved standing near, he said to his mother, 'Woman, behold, your son!' Then he said to the disciple, 'Behold, your mother!' And from that hour the disciple took her to his own home" (John 19:25–27).

The natural question here arises: If Mary did have other children besides Jesus, why would he entrust his mother into the care of someone not a member of the family? Saint John was the son of Zebedee. It doesn't make sense that Christ would have done this if he, in fact, had brothers who were sons of Mary.

Throughout all of the New Testament, only Christ is called the "son of Mary"—no one else is called that.

In Luke 2:41–51 we read about the "finding in the temple." The Holy Family went up to Jerusalem, and while there, Mary and Joseph became separated from Christ. There is no mention of other children, only Jesus. If Mary and Joseph had had other children, one would expect some mention of them here and could conclude from this silence that there were no other children.

Another important clue in this matter is what happened at the Annunciation, which is recounted in Luke 1:26–38. Mary's reaction to the Angel Gabriel's news that "you will conceive in your womb and bear a son" seems very odd. His message made her "greatly troubled," and she asked, "How can this be, since I do not know man?" (LXX). This is a euphemism for Mary's not being physically involved with the man to whom she was betrothed, Saint Joseph. Her reaction points to the possibility that she had taken a vow of perpetual virginity and was therefore justifiably troubled when an angel told her that she would soon become pregnant, in spite of her promise to God to remain a virgin even in marriage (something that was not common in those days, though it was not unheard of).

If Mary had *not* taken a vow of perpetual virginity—something some Church Fathers and later theologians believed that she had done[2]—and if she had planned to live with her husband as man and wife, with all that that entails, then her perplexity at the angel's message that she would soon conceive a child is inexplicable. After all, she was a young woman about to be married, and she knew how babies are made.

Further Reading: CCC, 411, 492–494

44

The Rosary: A Truly Biblical Prayer

Catholics around the world are familiar with the rosary, a series of five Our Fathers, each followed by ten Hail Marys and a Glory Be (each set is known as a "decade"), counted out on a string of beads known as a rosary.

Traditionally, there were three "mysteries" or themes that one would meditate upon while praying the rosary: the Sorrowful Mysteries, the Joyful Mysteries and the Glorious Mysteries. According to this pattern, the total number of Hail Marys prayed in one rosary (i.e., the three mysteries) is 150. This corresponds to the 150 psalms in the Old Testament, which were also recited aloud by pious Jews and, later, by Christians as a prayer of praise to God. In 2002 Pope John Paul II added the Luminous Mysteries.

The purpose of these themes is to help order the mind while praying, by focusing on particular episodes in the lives of Christ, our Lord and Savior, and Mary his mother, who is a model for all Christians. In fact, she was the very *first* Christian, and she was present with Christ in virtually all the major episodes of his life.

This ancient and powerful collection of prayers to Our Blessed Lady and her son Jesus Christ has graced the lives of countless

Catholics for centuries. But many are not aware that the prayers of the rosary, as well as the mysteries of the rosary upon which we meditate, are drawn almost entirely from the pages of the Bible.

The *Sorrowful Mysteries* comprise:

1. *The Agony in the Garden*, which is a meditation on the events described in Matthew 26:36–46, Mark 14:32–42 and Luke 22:39–46;

2. *The Scourging at the Pillar*, which focuses on Matthew 20:19, 27:26, Mark 15:15, Luke 23:21 and John 19:1;

3. *The Crowning with Thorns*, which is described in Matthew 27:29–30, Mark 15:16–20 and John 19:2–5;

4. *The Carrying of the Cross*, which we read about in Matthew 27:31–34, Mark 15:22–23, Luke 23:26–33 and John 19:16–17;

5. *The Crucifixion and Death of Christ on the Cross*, which is recounted in Matthew 27:45–56, Mark 15:33–41, Luke 23:44–49 and John 19:30–37.

The *Joyful Mysteries* are:

1. *The Annunciation* of the Angel Gabriel to the Blessed Virgin Mary, seen in Luke 1:26–38;
2. *The Visitation* of Our Lady to her cousin Elizabeth, described in Luke 1:39–45;
3. *The Nativity* of the Lord Jesus Christ, which we meditate upon in Matthew 1:25 and Luke 2:6–7;
4. *The Presentation* of Christ in the Temple, which is described in Luke 2:22–38;
5. *The Finding of Christ in the Temple*, which we read about in Luke 2:41–52.

The *Glorious Mysteries* are:

1. *The Resurrection of Christ*, which we meditate upon in Matthew 28:1–10, Mark 16:1–11, Luke 24:1–12 and John 20:1–8;

2. *The Ascension of Christ* into heaven, which is described in Mark 16:19 and Luke 24:50–51;

3. *The Descent of the Holy Spirit* (i.e., Pentecost), which we read about in Acts 2:1–12;

4. *The Assumption of Mary* into heaven, which is alluded to in Psalm 132:8 and Revelation 12:1–18;

5. *The Crowning of Mary* as Queen of Heaven, which is also alluded to in passages such as 1 Corinthians 9:25, 2 Timothy 4:8, James 1:12, 1 Peter 5:4, Revelation 2:10 and Revelation 12:1.

The more recent *Luminous Mysteries* are:

1. *The Baptism of the Lord*, which is found in Matthew 3:17, Mark 1:4–11, Luke 4:21, and John 1:29-34;

2. *The Wedding at Cana*, which we read about in John 2:1–11;

3. *The Proclamation of the Kingdom*, examples of which are contained in Mark 1:15, Mark 2:3–13 and Luke 7:47–48;

4. *The Transfiguration of Christ*, which is seen in Matthew 17:1–8 and Luke 9:35;

5. *The Institution of the Eucharist*, which we read about in Matthew 26:26–30, Mark 14:22–26 and Luke 22:14–20.

The prayers of the rosary are also drawn from Scripture. The Our Father is drawn from Matthew 6:9–13:

Our Father who art in heaven,

Hallowed be thy name.

Thy kingdom come.

Thy will be done,

    on earth as it is in heaven.

Give us this day our daily bread,

and forgive us our trespasses,

    as we also forgive those who trespass against us;

And lead us not into temptation,

    But deliver us from evil.

The first part of the Hail Mary is found in the greeting of the angel Gabriel to Mary in Luke 1:28, "*Hail, full of grace, the Lord is with you*" (emphasis added). The second part comes from Elizabeth's exclamation in Luke 1:42, "*Blessed are you among women, and blessed is the fruit of your womb!*" (emphasis added). The third part of the Hail Mary goes like this: "*Holy Mary, mother of God, pray for us sinners now and at the hour of our death, amen.*"

While this third part of the Hail Mary is not drawn directly from Scripture, it is surely consistent with the Bible's teachings. First, there is no doubt that Mary is holy. After all, God chose her to be the mother of the Second Person of the Blessed Trinity, the Incarnate Christ. As Mary herself said in Luke 1:46–53, she knew she was "lowly" but that God had "*exalted* those of low degree" (emphasis added). She understood that "all generations" would call her "blessed," which is a clear indication of her holiness.

Second, Mary was truly the Mother of God, since the person born to her, Jesus Christ, was God himself who had taken flesh for our salvation (John 1:1, 14). She was not the mother of just Christ's human nature (what mother shows off her newborn baby and says, "Look at the beautiful human *nature* I just gave birth to"?).

No, mothers give birth to *persons* who possess human natures. In Christ's case, he is a divine Person, who possesses the fullness of both a divine and a human nature. Elizabeth spoke the truth when she saw Mary coming to her: "And why is this granted to me, that *the mother of my Lord* should come to me?" (Luke 1:43, emphasis added).

And third, as a member of the body of Christ, Mary is also called by God to offer "supplications, prayers, intercessions, and thanksgivings…for all men…. This is good, and it is acceptable in the sight of God our Savior, who desires all men to be saved and to come to the knowledge of the truth" (1 Timothy 2:1–4).

If we are called by the Lord to pray for others, especially those who are most in need of our prayers, even more assuredly, the Blessed Virgin Mary, who is in heaven in the presence of the Blessed Trinity, will also be praying for us. She has been perfected in righteousness before God (Hebrews 12:23), and the Bible tells us that "the prayer of a righteous man [or woman!] has great power" (James 5:16).

So, when you pray the rosary, know that you are praying the most scriptural of prayers. Know also that when you pray the rosary with heartfelt love for God and a desire to draw ever closer to him, through the powerful intercession of the Blessed Virgin Mary, united with her Son Jesus Christ, he is well pleased (1 Timothy 2:3).

Further Reading: CCC, 2673–2682

45

Why Worry?

The Lord knows that in this life we're exposed to many people and situations that cause us to worry. After all, we don't call it a "vale of tears" for nothing.

Though Genesis 3 doesn't mention "anxiety" as one of the curses meted out to humanity as a result of Adam and Eve's original sin, it might as well have. The Bible's description of human events since our first parents were expelled from the Garden of Eden—the only worry-free zone mankind has ever known—is one long account of vexation, consternation and anxiety. In other words, it's the story of how sin affects us.

The truth is that sin breeds anxiety. It's like the legal catchphrase "Use a gun, go to jail." Especially when we've committed serious sins, we inevitably worry about what we've done. That's what our consciences are for: to alert us that something is wrong and, hopefully, to prompt us to remedy the situation through repentance. Many people are consumed with worries—not because their lot in life brings them unavoidable problems (as some people's lives do), but because they persist in doing things that are contrary to God's will for them. And their guilty conscience is like an alarm bell with no snooze button. It keeps rattling the soul, no matter how vigorously they try to block out the noise.

When unrepented sin infests your life, worries will multiply just as surely as flies leave maggots. In Sacred Scripture, the Lord teaches us that the cure for sin-induced worry is repentance and forgiveness. And, happily, just as sin causes worry, virtue subdues it. The life of a virtuous person is free of the worries caused by sin. What's more, the greater one's faith and hope in the Lord, the less one will be prey to anxiety caused by external things.

The following passages from Scripture show us that we shouldn't worry about things we can't control and that we are doomed to worry about the thing we *can* control, namely, sin. The message is: Live a good life, avoid sin, seek to do God's will and you'll be free of needless worry and anxiety.

Philippians **4:4–7** "Rejoice in the Lord always; again I will say, Rejoice. Let all men know your forbearance. The Lord is at hand. Have no anxiety about anything, but in everything by prayer and supplication with thanksgiving let your requests be made known to God. And the peace of God, which passes all understanding, will keep your hearts and your minds in Christ Jesus."

1 Peter **5:6–7** "Humble yourselves therefore under the mighty hand of God, that in due time he may exalt you. Cast all your anxieties on him, for he cares about you."

Psalm **94:17–19** "If the LORD had not been my help, / my soul would soon have dwelt in the land of silence. / When I thought, 'My foot slips,' / thy steadfast love, O LORD, held me up. / When the cares of my heart are many, / thy consolations cheer my soul."

Proverbs **12:25–28** "Anxiety in a man's heart weighs him down, / but a good word makes him glad. / A righteous man turns away from evil, / but the way of the wicked leads them astray. / A slothful man will not catch his prey, / but the diligent man will get precious wealth. / In the path of righteousness is life, / but the way of error leads to death."

Remember this: living a sinful life inevitably causes worry, anxiety and, eventually, leads to physical and spiritual *death*.

1 Maccabees 6:8–13 "When the king heard this news, he was astounded and badly shaken. He took to his bed and became sick from grief, because things had not turned out for him as he had planned. He lay there for many days, because deep grief continually gripped him, and he concluded that he was dying. So he called all his friends and said to them, 'Sleep departs from my eyes and I am downhearted with worry. I said to myself, "To what distress I have come! And into what a great flood I now am plunged! For I was kind and beloved in my power." But now I remember the evils I did in Jerusalem. I seized all her vessels of silver and gold; and I sent to destroy the inhabitants of Judah without good reason. I know that it is because of this that these evils have come upon me.'"

In Mark 4:13–20 (see also Luke 8:9–15), Christ explains to his disciples the meaning of the parable of the sower. Notice that one of the types of soil—the one covered in thorns—quickly choked off the seed that had been scattered there. One of these "thorns" Christ warns about is described as "the cares of the world." In other words, there are people who are so consumed with worry about the mundane details of life that the graces God wants to lavish on them go unused—indeed, are *made unusable*—because worry prevents them from ever taking root in the soul. He also warns that worry can so consume us that we risk being unprepared for his return, not to mention that day on which each of us will die and stand before him to be judged (Hebrews 9:27).

In Luke 21:34–36, Christ gives a strong warning: "But take heed to yourselves lest your hearts be weighed down with dissipation and drunkenness and cares of this life, and that day come upon you suddenly like a snare; for it will come upon all who dwell upon the face of the whole earth. But watch at all times, praying that you may have strength to escape all these things that will take place, and to stand before the Son of man."

There are times, of course, when worry is unavoidable. Saint Paul spoke several times about the anxiety he suffered on the behalf of his fellow Christians (2 Corinthians 11:28). The real issue, however, is how we *handle* our worries. Whether it's an unavoidable external trial or just needless anxiety we create for ourselves, we can choose to deal with the problem virtuously (i.e., by entrusting the problem with loving faith to God's fatherly providence). Remember Christ's consoling promise to us:

Therefore I tell you, do not be anxious about your life, what you shall eat or what you shall drink, nor about your body, what you shall put on. Is not life more than food, and the body more than clothing? Look at the birds of the air: they neither sow nor reap nor gather into barns, and yet your heavenly Father feeds them. Are you not of more value than they? And which of you by being anxious can add one cubit to his span of life? And why are you anxious about clothing? Consider the lilies of the field, how they grow; they neither toil nor spin; yet I tell you, even Solomon in all his glory was not arrayed like one of these. But if God so clothes the grass of the field, which today is alive and tomorrow is thrown into the oven, will he not much more clothe you, O men of little faith? Therefore do not be anxious, saying, "What shall we eat?" or "What shall we drink?" or "What shall we wear?" For the Gentiles seek all these things; and your heavenly Father knows that you need them all. But seek first his kingdom and his righteousness, and all these things shall be yours as well. Therefore do not be anxious about tomorrow, for tomorrow will be anxious for itself. Let the day's own trouble be sufficient for the day. (Matthew 6:25–34)

46

Love One Another

Christ said, "If you love me, you will keep my commandments" (John 14:15). He wasn't referring to love as a mere emotion, the syrupy, romanticized "love" that involves no suffering and demands no sacrifice. The kind of love Christ meant is *charity*: the steadfast, self-giving, humble, courageous, act-of-the-will love that seeks the good of our neighbor, even if it means sacrifice or suffering on our part.

True charity involves loving others who may not be particularly likeable, much less loveable, including those who don't reciprocate that love. In the face of your charity, some may be all the more hostile and resentful. But Christ calls you to love them nonetheless. This is the basis of the communion of saints; this bond of charity unites all the members of the body of Christ (Romans 12:3–6).

As we'll see in the following passages, each member of the body of Christ is called to seek the good of all the others.

John 13:34–35 "A new commandment I give to you, that you love one another; even as I have loved you, that you also love one another. By this all men will know that you are my disciples, if you have love for one another."

John 15:12–17 "This is my commandment, that you love one another as I have loved you. Greater love has no man than this, that a man lay down his life for his friends. You are my friends if you do what I command you.… This I command you, to love one another."

Notice that Christ specifically linked Simon Peter's profession of love for him ("Simon, do you love me?") with the command, "feed my sheep." And the Lord reminds all of us that charity for one another is second in importance only to loving God (Matthew 22:38; Mark 12:30–31, 1 Corinthians 13). This law of charity is emphasized in the New Testament at every turn, especially in the form of intercessory prayer.

Galatians 6:2 "Bear one another's burdens, and so [you will] fulfill the law of Christ."

Romans 12:10 "[L]ove one another with brotherly affection; outdo one another in showing honor.… [C]ontribute to the needs of the saints."

1 Corinthians 10:24 "Let no one should seek his own good, but the good of his neighbor."

1 Thessalonians 4:9–10 "But concerning love of the brethren you have no need to have any one write to you, for you yourselves have been taught by God to love one another.… But we exhort you, brethren, to do so more and more."

1 Thessalonians 5:11, 14–15 "Therefore encourage one another and build one another up.… And we exhort you, brethren, admonish the idle, encourage the fainthearted, help the weak…always seek to do good to one another and to all" (see 2 Corinthians 1:10–11).

Christ's law of love is a standing command for all in his Church. It doesn't matter whether a Christian is living here on earth or in heavenly glory, in the immediate presence of the Lord: all are still bound under Christ's command to "love one another." On earth we can carry this out through physical acts of charity (Matthew 25:31–46; James 2:14–17), as well as spiritual acts of charity, especially through intercessory prayer on behalf of others (1 Timothy 2:1–4).

Saint Paul exhorts Christians to pray, supplicate, petition and intercede for all people. He emphasizes that intercessory prayer "is good, and it is acceptable [some translations use pleasing] in the sight of God our Savior" (see 1 Timothy 2:1–4). Similar exhortations permeate the New Testament:

Romans 15:30 "I appeal to you, brethren, by our Lord Jesus Christ and by the love of the Spirit, to strive together with me in your prayers to God on my behalf."

2 Corinthians 1:10-11 "[O]n him [Jesus] we have set our hope that he will deliver us again. You also must help us by prayer, so that many will give thanks on our behalf for the blessing granted us in answer to many prayers."

Colossians 1:3, 9–10 "We always thank God, the Father of our Lord Jesus Christ, when we pray for you…. [W]e have not ceased to pray for you, asking that you may be filled with the knowledge of his will in all spiritual wisdom and understanding, to lead a life worthy of the Lord."

And here are some final thoughts from Saint Paul worth pondering: "[M]y heart's desire and prayer to God for them is that they may be saved" (Romans 10:1), and "I remember you constantly in my prayers. As I remember your tears, I long night and day to see you" (2 Timothy 1:3).

To those who argue that the saints in heaven do not pray for us, I would pose this question: In light of Saint Paul's intense desire to assist others through his prayers while on earth, is there any reason to imagine that upon entering heaven his charity and desire for others' salvation would be quenched and his prayers for others cease? Not at all. All members of the body of Christ, including those in heaven, practice charity.

And this is why we ask those in heaven to pray for us (1 Timothy 2:1–5).

Further Reading: Matthew 5:42–46; 19:19; Mark 12:28–14; Luke 6:27–36; Romans 12:9–13; Galatians 5:9–13; 6:2; Ephesians 4:4, 32; 1 Thessalonians 3:12; 4:9–10, 18; Hebrews 3:13; 1 John 4:7–21
CCC, 1822–1829, 1965–1974, 2093–2094

Notes

Introduction

1. Saint Jerome, *Commentary on Isaiah*, prologue, as quoted in CCC, 133. Saint Jerome lived circa AD 340–420.

Chapter 2
Temptations

1. Samuel Johnson, www.quotationspage.com/quotes/Samuel_Johnson/.

Chapter 7
Gossip, Slander and Judging People's Hearts

1. Doris Benardete, ed., *Mark Twain: Wit and Wisecracks* (Mount Vernon, N.Y.: Peter Pauper Press, 1998), p. 14.

Chapter 9
Humility

1. Aleksandr Solzhenitsyn, www.quotationspages.com.

Chapter 10
Homosexuality

1. See Genesis 19:1–29; Romans 1:24–27; 1 Corinthians 6:10; 1 Timothy 1:10.

Chapter 17

The Blessed Trinity

1.   Theophilus of Antioch, *Ad Autolycus*, 2,15, as cited in *The
     Faith of the Early Fathers*, William A. Jergens, ed. (Collegeville,
     Minn.: Liturgical Press, 1970), vol. 1, p. 75; Tertullian,
     Adversus Preaxeam, chapter 2, as cited in *Ante-Nicene Fathers*,
     Alexander Roberts and James Donaldson, eds. (Peabody,
     Mass.: Hendrickson, 1994), vol. 3, p. 598. See also Tertullian,
     On Modesty, 21, at http://www.newadvent.org/fathers/
     0407.html.

Chapter 20

Is It a Sin to Vote for Pro-Abortion Candidates?

1.   Congregation for the Doctrine of the Faith, no. 22
     (November 18, 1974), emphasis added. Available at
     www.vatican.va.

Chapter 21

Qualities of a Good Bishop

1.   Note that the clause "husband of one wife" does not mean
     that a bishop *must* be married, as some mistakenly imagine.
     It means that a man who had been remarried after the death
     of his wife could not be considered as a candidate for
     bishop. This ecclesiastical discipline was akin to celibacy in
     the priesthood.

2.   Saint Augustine, "Sermon 340," *Patrologia Latina* 38, 1438, as
     cited in *Lumen Gentium* IV: 32, *Vatican II: The Conciliar and
     Post Conciliar Documents*, Austin Flannery, O.P., ed. (Boston:
     St. Paul Books and Media, 1975), p. 390.

Chapter 24
Gluttony

1.   Saint Thomas Aquinas, *Summa Theologica*, III, art. 1, q. 148, p. 1 (Westminster: Christian Classics, 1981), p. 1787.

2.   Joseph F. Delaney, "Gluttony," *The Catholic Encyclopedia*, vol. 6 (New York: Robert Appleton Co., 1909), p. 590.

Chapter 25
Do Catholics "Keep Christ on the Cross"?

1.   Henry Nutcombe Oxenham, "The Child-Christ on the Cross," *The Oxford Book of English Mystical Verse*, D.H.S. Nicholson and A.H.E. Lee, eds. (Oxford: Clarendon Press, 1917), as quoted on www.bartleby.com.

Chapter 26
Purgatory

1.   Saint Augustine interpreted Matthew 12:32 in this way with regard to purgatory in *City of God*, 21:24:2.

Chapter 31
Infant Baptism

1.   See 2 Corinthians 5:17; 2 Peter 1:4; cf. Galatians 4:5–7. Cf. 1 Corinthians 6:15; 12:27; Romans 8:17.

2.   Patrick Madrid, *Answer Me This!* (Huntington, Ind.: Our Sunday Visitor, 2003), p. 185.

Chapter 33
The Divinity of Christ

1.   In Greek, *kurios mou kai ho theos mou,* which literally means "the Lord of me and the God of me."

Chapter 34
The Origin of Original Sin

1. Saint Augustine, *On Marriage and Concupiscence*, book 2, chapter 15: "For even as 'by one man sin entered into the world, and death by sin; so also has death passed through to all men, for in him all have sinned' (see Romans 5:12). *By the evil will of that one man all sinned in him, since all were that one man, from whom, therefore, they individually derived original sin*" (emphasis added); see also ibid. book 1, chapter 37; section 2, chapters 25 and 26. New Advent Online Patristics Library, http://www.newadvent.org/fathers/15072.htm.

Chapter 37
Don't Delay Conversion!

1. Thomas à Kempis, *The Imitation of Christ* 1, 23, 1, as cited in CCC, paragraph 1014.

2. Saint Francis of Assisi, *Canticle of the Creatures*, as quoted in CCC, paragraph 1014.

Chapter 38
The Myth of a "Total Apostasy"

1. Bruce R. McConkie, *Mormon Doctrine* (Salt Lake City: Bookcraft, 1966), pp. 43–44.

Chapter 39
The Field of Wheat and Weeds

1. Saint Thomas Aquinas, *Summa Theologica*, III, art. 8, q. 3 obj. 2.

CHAPTER 40

Lust and Impurity

1.   Saint Augustine, *Confessions*, 8:7, (London: Penguin, 1961),
     p. 169. The complete quote reads:"As a youth, I had been
     woefully at fault, particularly in early adolescence. I had
     prayed to you for chastity and said, 'Give me chastity and
     continence, but not yet.' For I was afraid that you
     would answer my prayer at once and cure me too soon of
     the disease of lust, which I wanted satisfied, not quelled."

CHAPTER 43

The "Brothers" of the Lord

1.   Although some modern translations use the term "kinsmen,"
     the literal rendering of Genesis 13:8, in the Hebrew, Greek
     and Latin, is "we are brethren" (*fratres enim sumus*).

2.   See Augustine, *On Holy Virginity*, 4.

Scripture Index

ABOUT THE AUTHOR

Patrick Madrid is the best-selling author of twelve books on Catholic themes including *Search and Rescue, Answer Me This!, Pope Fiction* and the acclaimed *Surprised by Truth* series. He hosts the Thursday edition of EWTN Radio's *Open Line* call-in radio show, is the host of four EWTN television series and edits www.envoymagazine.com, a print and digital magazine of Catholic apologetics and evangelization. A popular seminar presenter, Patrick has spoken at countless parishes, universities and conferences across North America, Europe, Asia and Latin America. He and his wife Nancy have been blessed with eleven happy and healthy children. For more information about his work, please visit www.patrickmadrid.com.